Western Philosophy
an introduction

by
R. J. Hollingdale

TAPLINGER PUBLISHING COMPANY
NEW YORK

First published in the United States in 1979 by
TAPLINGER PUBLISHING CO., INC.
New York, New York

Library of Congress Catalog Card Number: 79–63624
ISBN 0–8008–4206–5

190
H

Contents

1

Foreword

THE OBJECT of this little book is to introduce Western philosophy to the beginner. It is assumed that the reader has no knowledge of the subject but would like to acquire some.

Philosophy is not a science, although parts of it depend upon "scientific" exactitude; neither is it an art, although the "inspiration" associated with artistic creation often lies behind philosophical ideas. What philosophy *is* will be outlined in the preface which follows. The basic details of the subject are outlined in the two main parts: the introduction to its subject-matter and the introduction to its history. A knowledge of both is essential to a knowledge of the subject, and both are presented in as concise and elementary a way as is consistent with accuracy.

To make a beginning in any subject one needs to obtain a grasp of the matters with which it deals and then to orientate oneself in the practice and theories of the practitioners of that subject, past and present. To assist the beginner in philosophy to achieve this grasp and this orientation is the object of the present book.

Preface on the nature of philosophy

I

PHILOSOPHY IS a specialised study which must be learnt. But it has its origins in certain common needs of which people who are not philosophers are also conscious. Two are especially important.

Firstly, there is the need to explain. Children are always asking for explanations: they want to know the how, why and wherefore of everything they see which is unfamiliar. This intense curiosity usually wanes with advancing age, but very few lose it altogether. Even the least curious will experience moments of perplexity, and the most trusting will sometimes doubt. All thinking people will, at least now and then, feel dissatisfied with received opinion and will ask why this or that view or belief should be widely held and thought true. A philosopher is one who questions received opinion and seeks new solutions not now and then but as a full-time occupation.

Secondly, there is the need to decide. Throughout our lives we are faced with situations in which we have to make a decision: we have to choose this course of action or that. Failure to choose is itself a choice: we may choose not to choose; it is impossible to live and not make choices. This being so, we have a fundamental need to know how to make choices, to know why we should choose this and not that, and to understand how to relate our choices one to another. Since we do not live alone but in societies, we must also know how to understand the choices made by other people and how to relate our decisions to theirs. A philosopher is one who reflects on these things not now and then but systematically and as a life-task.

When we try to understand what the world is like—when we try to "explain" it—we are trying to discover what it "means", whether or not there is any purpose to be discovered in it, what sense, if any, can be made of it. The same is true when we consider the nature of choice and try to organise our choices systematically, for we cannot do this without at the same time asking ourselves what is important in life. So we may say that there exists in man a desire to establish "what life means", and that a philosopher is one in whom this desire is strong and whose activities are directed towards satisfying it.

How he goes about this task, and what conclusions he reaches, constitute the subject-matter of philosophy.

2

VIEWED ON the broadest scale, philosophising consists of two processes, which we may call evaluation and systematisation. A philosopher tries to assess the value and reliability of the knowledge we have, or think we have, about the world and ourselves, and of the beliefs we hold about the nature of the universe. He subjects them to logical tests to decide whether they are reasonable. And in doing so, he exposes that which is false or unreasonable in them. This process we may call the evaluation of knowledge.

Many philosophers have insisted that to subject knowledge to the test of logic is *all* a philosopher can do, and that whoever tries to do more than this fails to produce anything meaningful. Others, however, have considered it a function of philosophy to produce a coherent and consistent account of human thought and knowledge, to relate ideas to ideas and to organise them into a whole. This process we may call systematisation, and the endeavour to construct all-embracing philosophical systems forms a large part of the history of philosophy.

By evaluating our knowledge, views and beliefs, and then (in some cases) organising them into a coherent whole, a philosopher aims at arriving at a profounder comprehension of the nature of the world and of mankind.

3

THE SUBJECT-MATTER of philosophy consists not only of the conclusions which philosophers have arrived at, but more especially of the methods they employ in reaching conclusions. It is important to realise and to bear in mind all the time that there are no agreed conclusions in philosophy; consequently, no authorities or sacred texts. Everything not only may but must be questioned. What remains is the practice of philosophising, a method of dealing with problems.

To "philosophise" is to approach certain questions by means of a certain method. The nature of the philosophical questions will be outlined shortly, and they are not hard to grasp; but the nature of the philosophical method is less easy to describe and can be properly grasped only through performance. One can understand philosophy fully only by philosophising, and to entice others to think philosophically—that is, according to philosophical method—is the ultimate aim of every philosopher, who, although he may wish his conclusions to be accepted as true, will want even more that his hearers or readers should understand *why* they are true, should think the matter through with him and contradict him if they can: in short, he invites his audience to become philosophers themselves, to learn to live in the light of philosophy and to order their thoughts in a philosophical way.

What that way is should become apparent during the course of this book, and especially in the part devoted to the history of philosophy. But it may be of help, as a preliminary, to examine briefly in what respects the method and aims of philosophy differ from those of science and religion.

4

PHILOSOPHY DIFFERS from science in four principal ways. Firstly, it does not consist of a body of agreed conclusions. In the Greek world of the sixth century B.C., when philosophy originated, all theoretical studies were considered to be "philosophy", and the earliest philosophers inquired into matters which we should now consider the property of science. But when the various sciences—mathematics, physics, chemistry, biology, and, in our time, psychology and anthropology—developed a body of agreed conclusions, they split off from philosophy and became specialised branches of study in their own right. It is not impossible that other sciences will evolve out of the present subject-matter of philosophy: logic, for example, is on the way to becoming a science independent of other philosophical subjects. Philosophy can to this extent be called the originator of the sciences. And this fact explains why there exists no body of agreed conclusions in philosophy itself: when a conclusion is reached, it seems, we cease to call it philosophy. We should note too that much philosophical speculation is concerned with clear thinking, and this means essentially abolishing confusion and dispelling puzzles and problems. When this is done, one is left, not with a "conclusion", but with the disappearance of what was formerly considered a problem.

Secondly, science and philosophy differ in that the process of philosophising is itself part of the subject-matter of philosophy. When a scientist makes an experiment he is concerned with the conditions under which the experiment is made and, of course, with its outcome; but he assumes that his equipment is in order and that there is nothing wrong with his eyesight or with his brain. In philosophy, however, the process of thinking is itself at issue. The subject-matter of philosophy includes the process of philosophising.

Thirdly, science does not set itself up to explain why the world is as it is or to adjudicate on the end or aim of existence, whereas philosophy does claim to do so. The scientist tries to understand the physical world (or, in the case of the psychologist and anthropologist, the mental and human world) and by understanding it to master it. But he does not draw any ethical or teleological conclusions from his knowledge—that is, he does not judge whether the world is "right or wrong" or deduce any purpose or design, any end or aim, in the world. Much of philosophy *is*, however, concerned with ethics and with the question of the presence or absence of a universal purpose or design. One of the undoubted tasks of philosophy as traditionally understood is to advise us on how we ought to live, and this task is outside the sphere of science.

Finally, although the sciences are certainly distinct from philosophy, they are subservient to it in so far as the validity of any scientific method can be established only by philosophic method. That is to say, the validity of the individual sciences depends upon the validity of human reason and the laws of logic, and these lie outside the scope of any individual science and belong to the realm of philosophy.

5

THE ALTERNATIVE to philosophy usually suggested as satisfying the need to explain and the need to decide is religion. The distinction between religion and philosophy can be discerned most clearly in their respective methods of acquiring knowledge. In religion, one knows through revelation. Ultimate truths are acquired through inspiration. They cannot be proved true and one is asked to believe them true without proof. In philosophy, on the contrary, one is asked to "believe" nothing. All conclusions must be demonstrated; and although "inspiration" may occur—in the sense that a philosopher may have a sudden and unpremeditated intuition—this intuition must be subjected to the test of logic. Although not all religions require belief in God—Buddhism, for example, is an atheistic religion —all demand belief in what cannot be demonstrated. Whether religion is an adequate substitute for philosophy depends on subjective factors, principally on the strength of a believer's faith. Philosophers are, perhaps naturally, inclined to see intense faith as wilful blindness, or at least as unjustifiable avoidance of logical difficulty. Nietzsche defined faith as "not *wanting* to know what is true", and although this is an unnecessarily harsh judgment—implying as it does *deliberate* falsification and blindness on the part of the believer—it is a fact that faith does imply a refusal to examine every objection with a clear head. Moreover, faith can fail and certainty may change to uncertainty against the will of the believer. He must then turn to philosophy for what has failed him in religion. This failure of certainty cannot occur in a philosopher, partly because "certainties" are arrived at by stages whose strength has been tested step by step, but chiefly because philosophy is less a body of conclusions than a method of thinking.

6

THE WRITINGS of philosophers are sometimes so obscure, their terminology so peculiar and their conclusions so bizarre, that many people have come to think the whole subject a kind of intellectual game, rather like chess but even less amusing, and have asked whether the so-called problems of philosophy cannot be answered much more sensibly by means of man's natural intelligence or, as it is often called, his commonsense. The fallacy here is not so much that commonsense is rather uncommon, as that it is inadequate and represents in fact a sort of popularisation and simplification of what was once a philosophical discovery. Just as the theories of advanced physics of today develop into the commonplace objects of tomorrow, so the original speculations of a philosopher become the everyday common-place of later generations. Commonsense is therefore a consequence of philosophy and not an alternative to it. "Natural" intelligence, like every other "natural" quality, must be acquired, and it is through the speculations of philosophers that we acquire the intelligence which afterwards seems a natural gift.

7

PHILOSOPHY IS, then, a distinct discipline; and it would be wrong to suggest that there is any easy way of mastering it. To gain a proper understanding of any discipline is difficult, and only hard study will make it comprehensible. This is true of philosophy to a supreme degree. The student who embarks seriously upon it has ventured into something which will consume a large amount of his time and will, eventually, change his life. It is hard to think of any subject which, if seriously pursued, will bring about a profounder change in the student's outlook. Here is perhaps the basic distinction between philosophy and any other branch of study, religion alone excepted: a great physicist is asking you to change your ideas about the physical nature of the world, but a great philosopher is essentially asking you to change your life. As understanding of the subject deepens we become conscious of greater complexities and more subtle distinctions and we have to learn technical terms and disentangle intricate arguments. We have also to study the history of philosophy, where a great body of relevant thought opens up for us in the works of the great philosophers of the past. Some thinkers are difficult to understand, but there is no satisfactory short-cut to a proper assimilation of the ideas of the masters of philosophical reflection. However useful a summary may be in the early stages, there is no true substitute for the texts themselves, for only there can we find philosophy in all its fullness.

All this may seem daunting: but there is, of course, a way to begin, and the present book is devoted to it. It assumes that the reader is ignorant of philosophy but interested in finding out what it is and why it should be studied.

8

VIEWED AS a whole, philosophy presents a two-fold aspect. From one point of view, it is a number of specific areas of study which, taken together, make up the discipline of philosophy. From another, it is the history of speculation within these areas of study.

The history of philosophy is not, as in the case of other disciplines, a non-essential appendix to the main subject, but in a vital sense the subject itself. For example, the history of physics is of great interest to a physicist, but a knowledge of it is not essential to a knowledge of modern physics as such. "Physics" is a body of knowledge, "the history of physics" an account of how this knowledge was arrived at, and the two things are distinct. But there is a sense in which the "history of philosophy" and "philosophy" are one and the same thing, since the study of philosophy must consist in large part of a study of communicated thoughts on philosophical subjects, and these communicated thoughts constitute the history of philosophy. To emphasise the distinction in another way: the terms "physics" and "the writings of Newton, Einstein and other great physicists" are not equivalent in meaning; but the terms "philosophy" and "the writings of Plato, Aristotle, Kant, Hegel and other great philosophers" are nearly equivalent in meaning. To a far greater degree than in any other subject, the writings of the masters *constitute* the subject. Part Two of this book therefore offers a very brief history of philosophy as one of the two essential preliminaries to a study of the subject.

Now, it will be clear that the writings of philosophers must be *about* something, and what they are about will constitute the subject-matter of the study. The nature of this subject-matter can be analysed and arranged into different areas of study, and each area of study can be given an appropriate name. This codification of the subject-matter of philosophy was first carried out by Aristotle, and his classification is essentially the one still employed. It offers an approach to philosophy complementary to a study of its history, and if this approach is attempted first, the history will be more easily understandable. Part One of this book is therefore devoted to an exposition of the subject-matter of philosophy.

Part One

Introduction to the subject-matter of Western Philosophy

I   The departments of philosophy

THE SUBJECT-MATTER of philosophy is the basic problems upon which men are capable of reflecting. There are five such basic problems.

   i Reflection on the nature of reasoning.
   ii Reflection on the nature of knowledge.
   iii Reflection on the nature of being.
   iv Reflection on the nature of morality.
   v Reflection on the nature of beauty.

Each of these problems is the subject of a department of philosophy:

   i Theory of reasoning, or *logic*.
   ii Theory of knowledge, or *epistemology*.
   iii Theory of being, or *metaphysics*.
   iv Theory of morality, or *ethics*.
   v Theory of beauty, or *aesthetics*.

These departments are not self-contained, but overlap and influence one another. For example, a philosopher's metaphysics will influence his ethics, his views on logic will influence his views on the nature of knowledge. It is possible to combine ethics and aesthetics into a single theory of value. And so on.

Further, these departments can be applied to what we may call "practical philosophy", by which is meant the application of philosophical theory to the study of other subjects. Thus we can speak of political philosophy, philosophy of religion, philosophy of history, and so on.

2 Logic

LOGIC, OR theory of proof, is the theory of correct reasoning, and to that extent the basis of philosophy, which depends in all its branches upon correct reasoning. Expanding this definition a little, we can define logic as the theory of the conditions under which reasoning is or arguments are valid. Believing that one or more statements are true, we may infer from them that a third is true. The task of logic is to decide whether inferences are good or bad, to devise a system of distinguishing between good and bad inferences, and to give an account of the different kinds of valid argument and the connections between them.

Inference is a process by which we establish the truth of a sentence from the truth of other sentences which constitute the evidence for it. A "conclusive inference" is one that must be logically true if the reasons given are true; that is, it is logically impossible for the inference to be false. A "probable inference" is one which is not conclusive; that is, an inference which is probably, but not logically true, given the evidence.

There are two types of logic, called deductive and inductive. Deductive logic is the theory of conclusive inference, inductive logic the theory of probable inference. A deductive inference is an inference from general statements to a particular statement. One example of a deductive inference is: "All men are mortal, Socrates is a man, therefore Socrates is mortal." The third statement is a deductive inference from the first and second statements. It establishes a particular truth ("Socrates is mortal"). And the truth of this follows as a logical consequence of the first and second statements: if they are true, then the third must be true. An inductive inference is an inference from particular statements to a general statement. One example of an inductive inference is: "The sun rose this morning, the sun rose yesterday morning, there is no recorded instance of a day on which the sun did not rise, therefore the sun rises every day." The last statement is an inductive inference based upon the preceding statements. It follows from them as a probable consequence, but not as a certain or logical consequence—there is nothing in the preceding statements to make it logically necessary that the last be true. And the last statement establishes a probable general truth ("the sun rises every day") from statements of particular truths. Philosophers are concerned chiefly with deductive logic, and it is to this that we must devote most of our attention. The theory of inductive logic is complex and incapable of being stated simply. It is the method of science and the basis of probability theory and statistical analysis, subjects which cannot be dealt with as a sub-branch of philosophy. So-called "laws of nature" are examples of inductive inference, and the important point for the beginner in philosophy to grasp about such inferences is that, being inductive, they are not certainly true, but probably true. Essentially, an inductive inference—a general statement inferred from particular statements—can be disproved by a single particular instance to the contrary. For example, the "law" that all unsupported bodies falling towards the earth fall at the same rate, and that that rate is 32 feet per second per second, is a general induction from a mass of particular instances. It does not follow as a *logical* consequence of these instances, but as a *probable* consequence. And it could therefore be proved false by a single true instance to the contrary, that is, an instance of a body which did not fall at this rate. It is important when considering any argument to be clear whether the inference drawn is inductive or deductive, whether it is a probable consequence of the reasons given or a logical consequence. The way to clarity in this matter lies in understanding the nature of deductive logic, since if an argument is not deductive it must be either false or inductive.

2

THE SOUNDEST introduction to deductive logic is a detailed study of the form of argument called the syllogism. Mastery of the syllogism will prepare the beginner for other types of deductive reasoning and provide a basic exercise in the analysis of logical argument.

Let us begin with an example of a syllogism:

> All humans are mortal,
> All Englishmen are humans,
> Therefore all Englishmen are mortal.

This, it will be seen, is an argument comprising three sentences. The first and second sentences are called the premises, the third is called the conclusion. The widest definition of a syllogism is, therefore, that it is an argument comprising two premises and a conclusion.

If we look more closely at these sentences we shall notice that each is composed of four elements. In the terminology of logic, these elements are called the quantifier, the subject-term, the copula and the predicate-term. The subject-term is the entity about which an assertion is to be made. The predicate-term is the assertion made about the subject-term. The copula is the term connecting the subject and predicate terms. And the quantifier indicates how much of the subject-term, or how many of the things denoted by the subject-term, are referred to. In the example, the quantifier in each sentence is "all" and the copula is "are". (The copula in any sentence of a syllogism will always be a part of the verb "to be".) In the first premise, the subject-term is "humans" and the predicate-term "mortal"; in the second premise, the subject-term is "Englishmen" and the predicate-term "humans"; in the conclusion, the subject-term is "Englishmen" and the predicate-term "mortal". This form of sentence is called the standard form and all three sentences in a syllogism must be in this form. We can therefore redefine a syllogism as an argument which contains two premises and a conclusion, the premises and the conclusion being sentences of standard form.

A sentence in standard form will always be a declarative sentence—that is, a sentence which makes an assertion—of the subject-predicate type. It will always be a sentence in which the predicate-term asserts something about the subject-term. Other types of sentences—interrogative (which ask questions), imperative (which give commands) and optative (which express wishes)—are outside the province of logic, because logic is concerned with the truth or falsity of reasoning and only declarative sentences can be true or false.

3

THE PRACTICAL point of the syllogism is that many kinds of reasoning encountered in everyday life can be reduced to this syllogistic form. When they are reduced to this form it is possible to determine whether the syllogism evolved is valid. If it is valid, then the reasoning is correct. If it is not, the reasoning is false. There exist rules for determining whether or not a syllogism is valid and these will be set out shortly. As a preliminary, however, we must discuss the nature of a true syllogistic sentence: that is, its quality and quantity, the distribution of its terms and what is meant by the middle, major and minor term.

The sentences of a syllogism will be either affirmative or negative: that is, the predicate-term will affirm something about the subject-term or deny something about it. The affirmative or negative character of the sentence is called its quality. Thus the sentence "The radio is turned on" is of affirmative quality, "The radio is not turned on" of negative quality. To determine the quality of a sentence one must see whether the copula or the subject-term are modified by a negative word— "not" or "no". If they are so modified the sentence is of negative quality, if not, it is of affirmative quality. Thus, for example, the sentence "Apes are not humans" is of negative quality, because the predicate-term "humans" asserts a negative, "are not", about the subject-term "apes". The sentence "No apes are humans" is also of negative quality, because the predicate-term makes a negative assertion about the subject-term "apes". But the sentence "Apes are non-humans" is not of negative but of affirmative quality, because the predicate-term "non-humans" asserts something positive about the subject-term "apes", namely that they are non-humans, and the copula "are" is not modified by "not".

A sentence in a syllogism will also be universal or particular. A universal sentence is one in which something is asserted of all the entities denoted by the subject-term. A particular sentence is one in which something is asserted of some of the entities denoted by the subject-term. Thus, "All Englishmen are humans" is a universal sentence, "Some Englishmen are humans" a particular sentence. The universality or particularity of a sentence is called its quantity. There is a third quantity, singularity, which is the quantity of a sentence which refers to one individual. But for the purposes of logic, singular sentences can be understood as universal ones. The reason is that syllogistic logic has to do with relations between classes of things, and from the point of view of syllogistic theory, one individual thing can be considered as forming a class composed of one member. Thus the sentence "Jack is a gentleman" can be treated as of universal quantity. When the subject-term is not modified by a quantifier, the sentence is treated as of universal quantity unless good sense demands that it be considered particular. So, for example, in the sentence "Apes are non-humans", the subject-term "apes" obviously refers to all apes and the sentence is therefore of universal quantity; on the other hand, "Men are dying in battle" obviously demands the understood quantifier "some" and the sentence is therefore particular.

The sentences of a syllogism must therefore be declarative sentences of affirmative or negative quality and universal or particular quantity. This means that there are four, and only four, types of sentence dealt with by syllogistic logic: universal and affirmative sentences, universal and negative sentences, particular and affirmative sentences and particular and negative sentences. An example of a universal and affirmative sentence is "All Englishmen are humans"; of a universal and negative sentence "Apes are not humans"; of a particular and affirmative sentence "Some Englishmen are six feet tall"; and of a particular and negative sentence "Many men are not six feet tall". For the sake of brevity, these four types of sentences are designated by the letters A, E, I and O. Universal and affirmative sentences are called A-type sentences, universal and negative E-type, particular and affirmative I-type and particular and negative O-type.

The subject-term and predicate-term of a standard sentence will refer either to all the members of the class denoted or to some of them. In the former case, we say that the term is distributed. For example, in the sentence "All Englishmen are humans", the subject-term "Englishmen" is modified by the quantifier "all" and therefore denotes the entire class of Englishmen, and is therefore distributed. But in the case of "Some Englishmen are six feet tall", the subject-term does not denote the entire class of Englishmen, but only some of that class, and is therefore not distributed.

In an A-type sentence—e.g. "All Englishmen are humans"—the subject-term is distributed but the predicate-term is not distributed. The term "humans" denotes the class of human beings, and the sense of the example sentence is that the class of Englishmen is included in the class of human beings. Vice versa is not implied, as is evident if we reverse the terms and say "All humans are Englishmen", which is not an equivalent statement and demonstrates that the term "humans" does not denote all humans.

In an E-type sentence—e.g. "Apes are not humans"—subject and predicate terms are both distributed, since both terms denote an entire class. The sense of the example sentence is that the class of apes is excluded from the class of humans and vice versa is clearly implied, as is evident if we reverse the terms and say "No humans are apes", which is an equivalent statement.

In an I-type sentence—e.g. "Some Englishmen are six feet tall"—subject and predicate terms are both undistributed, since neither denotes an entire class. The sense of the example sentence is that the class of Englishmen and the class of things which are six feet tall share common members.

In an O-type sentence—e.g. "Many men are not six feet tall" —the subject-term is undistributed (many men, not all men) and the predicate-term is distributed. The sense of the example sentence is that many of the class of men are excluded from the class of things which are six feet tall; therefore, the predicate-term "six feet tall" denotes all six feet tall things and it is therefore distributed.

It will be seen that in universal sentences—types A and E— the subject-term is distributed and in particular sentences— types I and O—it is not distributed; and that in negative sentences—E and O—the predicate-term is distributed and in affirmative sentences—A and I—it is not distributed. A table will make these distinctions clear:

Sentence type	Subject-term	Predicate-term
A	Distributed	Not distributed
E	Distributed	Distributed
I	Not distributed	Not distributed
O	Not distributed	Distributed

In the example syllogism quoted at the beginning of the section there are three sentences—two premises and a con-clusion—each with a subject-term and a predicate-term. Thus there are six terms in all, three subjects and three predicates. But although there are six terms, there are only three *different* terms—"Englishmen", "humans" and "mortal"—each of which appears twice. One of these is called the middle term, one the major term and one the minor term. The middle term is the term which appears in both premises, the major term is the term which appears as the predicate of the conclusion, and the minor term is the term which appears as the subject of the conclusion. Thus, in the example syllogism, the middle term is "humans", the major term "mortal" and the minor term "Englishmen". For the sake of brevity, these three terms are designated by the letters M, P and S. The middle term is called the M-term, the major term the P-term and the minor term the

S-term. By means of these symbols, it is possible to state the example syllogism in abstract, general form, as follows:

All humans are mortal = All M are P,
All Englishmen are humans = All S are M,
Therefore, all Englishmen are mortal = Therefore, all S
are P.

The terms "major" and "minor" are also used to describe the premises: the major premise is the premise containing the major term, the minor premise is the premise containing the minor term. In the example, the major premise is "All humans are mortal", because "mortal", being the predicate of the conclusion, is the major term. The minor premise is "All Englishmen are humans", because "Englishmen", being the subject of the conclusion, is the minor term.

4

THERE ARE five rules for determining whether a syllogism is valid. If a syllogism violates any of these rules, it is invalid.

Rule One: The middle term must be distributed at least once. The middle term is the term which appears in both premises. A term is distributed when it refers to all the members of the class denoted by it. Violation of this rule is called the fallacy of undistributed middle. An example of a syllogism involving this error is:

All Englishmen are humans,
All Germans are humans,
Therefore all Germans are Englishmen.

(In symbolic notation: All P are M, All S are M, therefore all S are P). The major premise ("All Englishmen are humans") is an A-type sentence (i.e. universal and affirmative) and therefore its predicate "humans" is not distributed. The minor premise ("All Germans are humans") is also an A-type sentence and therefore its predicate "humans" is not distributed. Therefore the middle term is not distributed at least once. The consequence is that the middle term does not act as a connection between the two premises, and therefore the conclusion cannot follow from them.

Rule Two: If a term is not distributed in the premises, it must not be distributed in the conclusion. Violation of this rule is called the fallacy of illicit distribution. An example of a syllogism involving this error is:

> All Englishmen are humans,
> No Germans are Englishmen,
> Therefore no Germans are humans.

(In symbolic notation: All M are P, no S are M, therefore no S are P). The major premise ("All Englishmen are humans") is an A-type sentence (i.e. universal and affirmative) and therefore its predicate "humans" is not distributed. The conclusion ("No Germans are humans") is an E-type sentence (i.e. universal and negative) and therefore its predicate "humans" is distributed. Therefore the term "humans" is not distributed in one of the premises, but is distributed in the conclusion. The consequence is that the conclusion contains an element which cannot be derived from the premises: it refers to *all* humans, whereas the premises refer only to *some* humans.

Rule Three: No conclusion can follow from two negative premises. An example of a syllogism which violates this rule is:

> No non-humans are fair-haired,
> No Englishmen are non-humans,
> Therefore no Englishmen are fair-haired.

(In symbolic notation: No M are P, no S are M, therefore no S are P). Both premises are negative, therefore the terms "Englishmen", "non-humans" and "fair-haired" are not connected, therefore no conclusion can follow from them. To establish the conclusion we should have to show that "Englishmen" is included in the class of non-humans (none of which is fair-haired) and we in fact assert the reverse.

Rule Four: If either premise is negative, the conclusion must be negative. An example of a syllogism which violates this rule is:

> All Englishmen are white-skinned,

Some Russians are not white-skinned,
Therefore some Russians are Englishmen.

(In symbolic notation: All P are M, some S are not M, therefore some S are P). The major premise is affirmative, the minor premise negative, therefore the conclusion must also be negative. The correct conclusion from the given premises is "Some Russians are not Englishmen"—i.e. All P are M, some S are not M, therefore some S are not P.

Rule Five: A negative conclusion cannot follow from two affirmative premises. An example of a syllogism which violates this rule is:

All Englishmen are humans,
All humans are mortal,
Therefore some mortal things are not Englishmen.

(In symbolic notation: All P are M, all M are S, therefore some S are not P). Both premises are affirmative, therefore the conclusion must also be affirmative. A negative conclusion introduces data which is not derivable from the premises, which state no more than that all Englishmen are mortal. They do not state anything further about mortal things, therefore they do not state that there are some mortal things which are not Englishmen.

5

BY APPLYING the five rules given above to sentences in standard form, it is possible to decide whether an argument based upon them is valid or not. But such sentences are not met with very often in everyday life, and the sentences of common speech must be translated into logical form before the rules of logic can be applied to them. Bearing in mind that only declarative sentences can be true or false, and that therefore only this kind of sentence can be the subject of logical analysis, the translation of the terms of ordinary speech into standard sentences of A, E, I or O type is not very difficult. The technique is to rephrase common-speech sentences in the form: quantifier, subject-term, copula, predicate-term. There are some simple rules for doing this.

1. Be sure subject and predicate are in the correct order.

2. Identify subject and predicate when these are obscure. In the sentence "They love God who love their neighbour", it is not immediately obvious, which term is the subject and which the predicate. If, however, we translate the word "they" into "all persons", it becomes clear that the logical form of the sentence is "All persons who love their neighbour are persons who love God".

3. If the quantifier is missing, supply it. The rule is that "all" should be added unless "some" is clearly intended.

4. Where a complement is missing, supply it. Many declarative sentences employ a descriptive word or phrase where standard form needs to refer to classes. It is therefore necessary to add a complement to these descriptive words or phrases. For example, "Roses are red" should be rephrased "Roses are red flowers" or, more generally, "Roses are red things".

5. Where the copula is missing, supply it. In every standard sentence, subject and predicate terms must be connected by the copula "are" or "is". Where this is missing in a declarative sentence it should be inserted. For example, "Fish swim" should be rephrased "All fish are creatures which swim".

6. In the case of exclusive sentences—those which begin with "only", "none but" or similar phrases—replace the excluding word or phrase with "all" and reverse the order of subject and predicate terms. "None but the brave deserve the fair" is equivalent to "None but brave persons are persons who deserve fair persons" and this is equivalent to "All persons who deserve fair persons are brave persons", which is in standard form.

7. In the case of negative sentences—those which begin with "nothing", "none", "no one" and similar terms—replace the negating term with "no". For example: "Nothing evil can prosper" should be rephrased "No evil thing is a

thing which can prosper", which is a standard sentence.

8. In the case of a sentence in the form "all . . . are not", the rule is to treat it as an O-type sentence (i.e. particular and negative) unless an E-type sentence (i.e. universal and negative) is clearly indicated. For example, the sentence "All men are not fat" could, grammatically, mean that no men are fat, but obviously in fact means that some men are fat and some are not fat. It should therefore be treated as an O-type sentence.

9. In the case of exceptive sentences—those containing the word "except"—the rule is to treat them as A-type or E-type sentences. For example, the sentence "All birds can fly except ostriches" contains two meanings: "All birds which are not ostriches can fly" and "Ostriches cannot fly". The former is an A-type sentence ("All birds which are not ostriches are birds which can fly", universal and affirmative), the latter an E-type sentence ("No ostrich is a bird which can fly", universal and negative). A syllogism cannot contain two sentences to express a single premise, so the rule is to use one or the other, since if the argument is valid when one is used it will be valid if the other is used.

10. In the case of sentences containing the words "anyone", "anything", "if . . . then", "the", "whatever" and "whoever", the rule is to rephrase them as A-type sentences. For example, "Anyone who breaks the law will be punished" should be rephrased "All persons who break the law are persons who will be punished".

11. In the case of sentences containing the words "someone" or "something", the rule is to rephrase them as I-type sentences (i.e. particular and affirmative). For example, "Someone's in the kitchen" should be rephrased "Some persons are persons who are in the kitchen".

6

THESE RULES are for translating into standard form sentences not in that form so that they can be employed in a syllogism. It will be remembered that a syllogism can contain only three terms, each used twice; and it can happen that when the sentences of an argument have been put into standard form and arranged as two premises and a conclusion they will contain more than three terms and will therefore still not constitute a true syllogism. The technique of creating "equivalent sentences" exists to deal with this difficulty. An equivalent sentence is a sentence equivalent in meaning to another sentence but in a different logical form. By changing the logical form of a sentence we can reduce the number of terms and so create a true syllogism. The three possible means of doing this are obversion, conversion and contraposition.

Obversion involves changing the quality of a sentence and then negativing its predicate-term. For example: "No Englishmen are immortal", becomes "All Englishmen are immortal", then "All Englishmen are not immortal", which is equivalent to "All Englishmen are mortal". This last sentence is the equivalent sentence to "No Englishmen are immortal" and can be substituted for it. All types of logical sentences, A, E, I and O, can be obverted.

Conversion involves the interchange of subject-term and predicate-term. For example: "No apes are humans" becomes "No humans are apes". Only E-type and I-type sentences can be converted: e.g. "No Englishmen are Germans" (E-type, universal and negative) can be converted to "No Germans are Englishmen", and "Some Englishmen are crooks" (I-type, particular and affirmative) can be converted to "Some crooks are Englishmen". An A-type sentence (universal and affirmative) can be partially converted; in which case it is transformed into an I-type sentence: e.g. "All Englishmen are humans" can be partially converted to "Some humans are Englishmen". An O-type sentence (particular and negative) cannot be converted at all : e.g. "Some Englishmen are not crooks" is not equivalent to "Some crooks are not Englishmen".

Contraposition involves obverting a sentence, then converting the resultant sentence, then obverting the third sentence. For example: "All Englishmen are humans" is obverted to "No Englishmen are non-humans"; this sentence is converted to "No non-humans are Englishmen"; then this sentence is obverted to "All non-humans are non-Englishmen". A-type and O-type sentences can be contraposed, E-type can be partially contraposed, I-type cannot be contraposed.

7

IT WILL be useful to summarise in the briefest form the basic facts just discussed.

1. There are two kinds of inference, conclusive and probable, consequently two kinds of logic, deductive and inductive. Deductive logic is concerned with conclusive inference, inductive logic with probable inference. Deductive logic establishes particular truths from general truths, inductive logic general truths from particular truths.

2. Inductive logic is the method of science. The "laws of nature" and the so-called "deductions" of Sherlock Holmes and other fictional detectives are inductive inferences. Inductive logic has to do with establishing the probable facts of the actual world. Deductive logic is "pure" logic, concerned with establishing the conditions under which a certain statement is a conclusive inference from other statements. It does not establish facts about the actual world but only about logical connections between statements. The classic form of deductive logic is the syllogism.

3. a. A syllogism is an argument comprising three sentences: two premises and a conclusion. Each of the sentences is in standard form: that is, it is a declarative sentence composed of a quantifier, a subject-term, a copula and a predicate-term.

b.   These sentences are i of affirmative or negative quality, ii of universal or particular quantity, iii distributed or undistributed.

c.   They contain three terms in all: i the major, ii the minor, iii the middle term. The premise containing the major term is called the major premise, that containing the minor term is called the minor premise.

4.   There are five rules for determining whether a syllogism is valid: 1. The middle term must be distributed at least once. 2. If a term is not distributed in the premises, it must not be distributed in the conclusion. 3. No conclusion can follow from two negative premises. 4. If either premise is negative, the conclusion must be negative. 5. A negative conclusion cannot follow from two affirmative premises.

5.   Only sentences of standard form can be the subject of logical analysis. Therefore sentences in other forms must be transposed into standard form before they can be treated.

6.   When the sentences of an argument have been put into standard form they may still contain more than three terms and will therefore not constitute a true syllogism. To reduce the number of terms to three, one creates "equivalent sentences" by i obversion, ii conversion, iii contraposition.

8

FOR THE beginner to master the syllogism and the technique of reducing appropriate arguments to syllogistic form and criticising them in this form is a big step towards understanding logical theory. To attempt more than this as a beginning in logic would perhaps be to risk early discouragement. However, it is clearly sensible for the beginner to have an idea of the further steps in logic which lie ahead of him and perhaps to have his appetite whetted for them. The following brief notes on symbolic and propositional logic are intended to do no more than that.

The syllogism is the core of logical theory as devised by Aristotle and employed from his time until the beginning of the present century. We may call it "classical logic" to distinguish it from "modern logic", which represents the greatest clear advance in philosophical theory made during the present age. The distinction between classical and modern logic is, briefly, that classical logic is a logic of classes and modern logic is a logic of propositions. Both kinds may be expressed symbolically, but in classical logic symbolic notation is no more than a convenience whereas in modern logic symbolic notation is as much a necessity as it is in algebra.

We have already seen that a simple syllogism such as "All humans are mortal, all Englishmen are humans, therefore all Englishmen are mortal" can be expressed in symbolic form as "All M are P, all S are M, therefore all S are P". These symbols are called "variables", which means symbols which can stand for any word or phrase, and in the above example each variable stands for a class: S stands for "the class of Englishmen", M for "the class of humans", P for "the class of mortal creatures". Now, in the logic of propositions, the variables employed stand, not for classes, but for propositions; that is, for complete declarative sentences.

Thus the sentence "All Englishmen are humans" could be expressed by a single variable "p", which stands for the entire sentence.

To demonstrate the uses of this kind of symbolism let us take a slightly more complex syllogism than those we have been treating: "If 2 plus 2 is not equal to 4, then the rules of arithmetic are not accurate. But the rules of arithmetic are accurate. Therefore 2 plus 2 is equal to 4." If we replace the proposition "2 plus 2 is equal to 4" by the variable "p", and the proposition "the rules of arithmetic are accurate" by the variable "q", we can rephrase the argument in symbolic form as: "If, if not-p then not-q, and q, then p."

This is called the "argument form" of the concrete argument it stands for. And since this form is valid, it will remain true whatever propositions we put in place of p and q.

Symbolic logic also employs symbols to designate the words or phrases which connect the propositions. These symbols are called "propositional connectives" and in the above argument form there are three of them: "if . . . then", "not" and "and". These are usually designated in the following way: "if . . . then" by " ⊃ ", "not" by "∼", and "and" by a point, ".". Further, the scope of each of these propositional connectives is indicated by brackets. Employing these devices, we can rephrase the argument: "if, if not-p then not-q, and q, then p", as: "((∼p ⊃ ∼q) . q) ⊃ p".

A fourth propositional connective is "v", meaning "either . . . or, or both": "p v q" means "either p or q or both p and q are true".

Arguments which can be rephrased in an argument form of the kind given in the example are the subject-matter of the logic of propositions. But there are many arguments which cannot be correctly represented in this form, and a more complex procedure is required to deal with them. Specifically, more symbols are needed: the variables x, y, z, etc. to denote individuals: predicate symbols F, G, H, etc.; and the quantifiers "(x)", meaning "for all x's", and "(Ex)", meaning "there is an x such that. . . ." These additional signs are needed to formalise, for example, this simple syllogism: "If no philosophers are rich, and some Englishmen are philosophers, then some Englishmen are not rich". The appropriate formula is:

$$\text{"}((x)(Fx \supset \sim Gx).(Ex)(Hx.Fx)) \supset (Ex)(Hx.\sim Gx)\text{"}$$

In this formula, F = philosopher, G = rich and H = Englishmen. Retaining only the symbolic "x", meaning an individual, the formula can be rephrased in words as follows:

"If, for all x's, if x is a philosopher, then x is not rich; and there is an x such that x is an Englishman and x is a philosopher; then there is an x such that x is an Englishman and x is not rich".

The object of this symbolic logic is to eliminate from any argument that which is peculiar to it and to reduce it to its general logical form.

Epistemology

ONE OF the tasks of philosophy is to inquire into the nature of knowledge. To this inquiry belong such questions as: What conditions must obtain before we can be certain that the knowledge we have is true knowledge? Or can we never really be certain? Can we obtain knowledge from observation and experiment, or is all such knowledge really guesswork and not certain knowledge? Can we arrive at certain knowledge by pure thinking divorced from observation and experiment? How much of what we suppose to be knowledge is actually no more than supposition? Are there any subjects with which reason is incapable of dealing and about which which we can never acquire certain knowledge? This field of inquiry is called epistemology, or theory of knowledge (Greek "episteme" = knowledge or science), which may be defined as the theory of the nature of knowing and the means by which we know.

2

IT IS not immediately self-evident that knowledge really is a problem: to the "plain man" it may seem that either we know something or we do not know it. Let us therefore see, by means of some examples, in what way knowledge is problematical.

The first difficulty arises from the opinion we have just attributed to the "plain man": that we either know something or we do not know it. This opinion is quite true and logically unassailable—and therein lies the difficulty: it makes no sense to say that we "know mistakenly", yet the possibility is always present that we may be mistaken. In fields other than knowledge—in remembering, estimating, holding an opinion, and so on—we may legitimately confess to having been in error. We may "remember" something and later discover our memory was at fault, in which case we can say that we "remembered incorrectly". We may estimate the height of a tower at 100 feet and when we come to measure it find it to be 110 feet, in which case we can say that we "made a false estimate". We may hold an opinion which later knowledge shows to be unwarranted, in which case we can say that we were "mistaken in our opinion". But before our memory, estimate or belief was shown to be mistaken, we would probably have said that we "knew" facts later proved not to be facts: now we must admit that we did not "know" these facts. Clearly, if we use the word "know" correctly, we should use it only when the possibility of error is excluded: but how can we *know* that we might not be in error? This is the initial problem which faces anyone who begins to think about the nature of knowledge.

It may seem that a source of certain knowledge is observation of the world around us, that in sense impressions we possess an infallible source of information. But everyone will know of cases in which sense impressions have proved unreliable: the mirage in the desert is an obvious and quite valid instance of "seeing" something which in fact does not exist. There are many other, more common, instances. If we lower a straight stick into water, it seems to bend; if we take it out again, it seems to straighten. We "know" that the stick has not really changed its shape at all, but we do not "know" this from observation: so far as our eyes are concerned, a straight stick bends when lowered into water. In this matter, then, our eyes are deceived, and are not a reliable source of information.

But to convict our eyes of deceiving us we do not need even to lower the stick into water. We know already that the stick is not really straight but only appears straight because its indentations and curves are too slight to be visible without magnification. We can have demonstrated to us that no particular thing is absolutely straight, but we cannot *see* that this is true: to our eyes, many things seem straight. We may also believe that there is such a thing as a perfect circle, and even that we see perfect circles every day: but again we shall understand that in reality there are no perfect circles, and that again our eyes have deceived us.

Similar objections can be raised to the evidence of the other senses. Time and again they provide us with information that turns out to be false. It seems that the certainty we are seeking cannot be found through them.

A further example is provided by dreams. How do we know whether we are awake or dreaming that we are awake? Of course, writing these words I have no reasonable doubt that I am in fact awake. But may I not dream tonight that I am writing them, and may this dream not be every bit as real as this waking experience? If it be allowed that this *could* happen, what evidence can I produce which will suffice to *prove* that I am now awake and writing, and not rather in bed asleep and dreaming that I am awake and writing? Everyone will have experienced dreams which, at the time of dreaming, seemed to bear all the characteristics of actuality; and many people carry with them memories of experiences concerning which they cannot decide whether they occurred in actuality or in a dream. We are not speaking now about what is probably true, nor about whether, if life were a dream, this fact would make any practical difference. We are asking the question whether we have any way of knowing for certain whether we are, at any given moment, awake or asleep. If we cannot answer this question, we throw doubt on the reliability of our perceptions.

Let us look at the problem from another viewpoint. Suppose we trust the impressions our senses give us in those cases in which these impressions cannot be proved false—and in everyday life we are, of course, bound to trust our sense impressions most of the time: can we derive from them any certain knowledge which transcends sense impression? An example will make clear what is meant. We see a fire and feel heat. We say that the fire is the cause of the heat. How do we know this? We cannot see "fire causing heat", since "fire causing heat" is not a visible object, or an object of sense impression of any kind. It is, in fact, an inference. What happens is this: we experience A (in this case, fire), and then we experience B (in this case, heat); whenever we experience A we also experience B, and on no occasion when we experience A do we fail to experience B; and we always experience A and B in that order and not in the reverse order; and we therefore say that A has "caused" B. But this causation is not observed: we experience only A (fire) and B (heat), and no third phenomenon C (fire causing heat); phenomenon C is inferred from the observed relations between A and B. This inference is inductive and is therefore only probably true, not logically inevitable. It is derived from observation, and further observation *might* prove it false. We are therefore in no position to say that our inference "A causes B" is certainly true. This consideration applies to all knowledge inferred from sense impressions: even if we can be sure our sense impressions are accurate, we cannot be sure that the inferences we draw from them are true.

A form of knowledge apparently free from these limitations is deductive logic and mathematical knowledge. In this case, certain knowledge seems to be attainable: the conclusion of a valid syllogism is true, beyond any doubt. But the certainty attainable through deductive logic is gained at the cost of a divorce from everyday life and from the actual world. A syllogism can tell us nothing about what really exists. It speaks only of itself and of its own terms. An argument of the form "If, if not-p then not-q, and q, then p" is valid whatever propositions we put in place of "p" and "q", but it cannot tell us whether these propositions are true or false: it can give us no information about the actual world. This is also the case in geometry and trigonometry, which are concerned entirely with *ideal* figures—perfect circles, straight lines, equilateral triangles, and so forth, which, as we know, have no counterpart in the real world and cannot even be drawn. The conclusions in all these cases are of the "if . . . then" variety. For example, *if* the sides of a triangle are of equal length, *then* the angles at which they meet will be equal and the sum of these angles will be 180 degrees. But it is understood that in the real world there is no such thing as an equilateral triangle and that a drawing of one is only a crude approximation to the unattainable ideal. Deductive logic therefore can tell us what conclusions follow *if* certain propositions are true, but it cannot tell us *whether* they are true.

From yet another perspective, theory of knowledge has to inquire, not only what we know, but why: why "knowledge" at all? Clearly we have no "organ of knowledge" as we have an organ of digestion, we are not compelled to know as we are compelled to breathe: yet the need to know seems to be as ineradicable and "natural" as the need to breathe and digest. Or is this need in reality a need, not for knowledge, but for something else—security, for instance, or growth and expansion? Is "knowledge" only an instrument, and our search for knowledge a search for the most efficient instrument and not at all an attempt to discover "the nature of reality"? Certain typical characteristics of our "knowledge" suggest that these questions are not misdirected: we know that fire causes heat so as not to get burned, and this knowledge survives our discovery that we do not know any such thing—it is the not getting burned which weighs with us, and not any "search for the nature of reality"; we know that the sum of the angles of an equilateral triangle is 180 degrees, and we continue to know this even when we have understood that in reality equilateral triangles do not exist—here our need is for a simplification of reality, not an understanding of it, and this is also the case when we posit the existence of straight lines and circles. In these instances, an unpredictable and impossibly complicated world is rendered predictable and calculable: perhaps that is the purpose, the "why" of all knowledge.

To summarise: knowledge of the world is inferential knowledge; but how do we know that our inferences are based on correct and not mistaken sense impressions? and if our sense impressions are correct, how do we know that the inferences we draw are themselves correct? We can make a mistake in remembering, estimating and in an opinion: but we cannot sensibly say that we "know mistakenly"; either we know or we do not know. The problem is: how can we know *that* we know and *what* we know? It is to this problem that the branch of philosophy called epistemology addresses itself.

---

4   Metaphysics

1

BY THE broadest definition, metaphysics is the study of the basic structure of existence and of the nature of being. It can also be defined as the study of those things which transcend experience, or as a theory of the first principles or ultimate truths of the universe. In general, any philosophy which purports to "get down to fundamentals" and to describe the nature of life and the world as a whole, or which speculates about the aim of existence, may be called metaphysical.

2

THE QUESTIONS considered by this department of philosophy fall
into three big groups: i questions about the nature of God and
being, ii questions about the nature of mankind, iii questions
about the nature of the world. We shall consider first the two
fundamental questions of group iii: the questions of
permanence and change and of mind and matter. Then the
principal question of group ii: the question of freewill and
determinism. Finally we shall look briefly at the problems raised
in group i: the nature of God and of being. Before venturing
on these, however, we must consider something unique to
metaphysics among the departments of philosophy: the
question whether this department has any real right to exist at
all.

3

THE PARADOX of metaphysics is that many dispute its right to
exist, yet there seem to be real problems which can properly
be called metaphysical. The argument that metaphysical propositions are not meaningful can be stated as follows: only
empirical or analytic propositions are meaningful; but metaphysical propositions are neither empirical nor analytic;
therefore they are not meaningful. An empirical proposition is
a proposition which can be confirmed or refuted by observation
or experiment. For example, "London buses are red" is an
empirical proposition, since it can be confirmed or refuted by
going to London and looking at the buses there. Another
example is "Water boils at 100 degrees Centigrade", which can
be confirmed by taking the temperature of boiling water. An
analytic proposition is a proposition whose negation is self-
contradictory. For example, "All mothers are female" is an
analytic proposition, since the idea of "female" is contained in
the idea "mother"—which means "a female parent"—and therefore its negative, "All mothers are not female", is a self-contradiction. Another example is "At nightime there is no sunlight",

of which the negative, "At nightime there is sunlight", is self-contradictory, since the concept "no sunlight" is contained in the concept "night", which means "the period between sunset and sunrise". Now consider one of the grand metaphysical problems: for example, "Has man freewill?" Is either of the two possible answers to this question—"Man has freewill" and "Man has not freewill"—an empirical proposition? No, for neither can be confirmed or refuted by observation or experiment. Is either of them an analytic proposition? No, for the negative of neither is self-contradictory—i.e. the concept "freewill" is not contained in the concept "man". Since they are neither empirical nor analytic propositions they are not meaningful, and therefore the whole "problem" is meaningless.

The reply to this argument—that there exists a class of propositions which are neither empirical nor analytic in the sense in which the terms are defined above, but which nevertheless are meaningful—will be considered in Part Two, especially in the section devoted to Immanuel Kant. Here let it suffice to say that, to the "plain man" already referred to, it must seem that philosophers *ought* to be capable of finding meaning in the most pressing questions of life and that it would be a poor lookout for philosophy if they could not (and a poor lookout for mankind too, in so far as philosophy represents mankind's thinking ability at its greatest potential). We are born apparently out of nothing, and it must occur to us to ask why. We exist for a certain period of time, and we should be dull-minded indeed if we did not ask what existence really is, and what time is. We observe the universe around us and that there is much in it which *looks like* purposeful design, and we must ask whether any purpose really does reside in it. These and similar questions seem to be real and not pseudo-questions, even if they are at present (or perhaps for ever) unanswerable.

The division of opinion indicated above is very marked in contemporary philosophy; and we must also note that, quite apart from this deep division, there has always existed a marked scepticism concerning metaphysical discoveries. The grounds for this are fairly obvious. Metaphysics makes very big claims and deals with subjects which are held to be basic to all existence. Fame and notoriety are more easily obtained through the construction of exciting metaphysical systems than through any other philosophical activity. It is a dangerously attractive subject, and in no other is it so easy to be led into excesses and flights of fancy. One does not need to reject metaphysics altogether to be convinced that much in metaphysics is illusory; and this opinion is the basis of a division within the subject between what may be called positive metaphysicians and critical metaphysicians: the latter attempt to define, in metaphysical terms, the limits of the subject which may be crossed by the former only at the risk of writing nonsense.

Setting the problem of the validity of the subject aside for the present, let us now look at some of the principal questions with which metaphysicians are traditionally concerned.

Let us begin with the oldest of all metaphysical problems; that is, the first problem to enter the mind of man which is now counted part of the subject-matter of metaphysics: the problem of permanence and change.

It is characteristic of many metaphysical problems that they arise from the existence, or apparent existence, in the world of two features which are mutually incompatible, and the problem of permanence and change is of this kind. We cannot fail to notice that the world is changing, and the more closely we observe this change, the more likely we are to come to the conclusion that it involves everything and is perpetual; that there is no permanent state anywhere. On the other hand, it seems that there must be unchanging elements in the world, or we should not be able to recognise what are in fact familiar objects. The problem therefore is this: if everything changes, as it seems to do, how can anything be permanent? But if there are permanent elements in the world, as there seem to be, how can they be part of a world which is always changing?

Early solutions of this problem (which we shall discuss in Part Two) involved: (i) emphasising change at the expense of permanence, (ii) emphasising permanence at the expense of change, (iii) reconciling change and permanence by suggesting that the world is composed of unchanging but invisible elements whose combinations and separations produce visible change. The third theory provided the conceptual basis of seventeenth century atomistic science and consequently of modern atomic physics. A further solution to the problem was to suggest that an eternal, unchanging world of "ideal" objects exists, of which the "apparent" world of material objects is a sort of reflection—a theory which became very influential in the form of a theory of a "real" and an "apparent" world. This kind of process—the evolution of a far-reaching and far from obvious theory of existence out of a simple observation concerning the actual world—is a notable characteristic of metaphysics.

The problem of permanence and change is a problem posed by the actual world considered chiefly as a world of material substance. But the world does not only contain physical matter; it also contains mind; and the existence, or apparent existence, of these two features—mind and matter—is another instance of mutually incompatible phenomena.

The world as we know it seems to be divided into two distinct parts: the world of matter and the world of mind. There exists the physical world, which consists of all material objects, visible and invisible, including our own bodies; and the mental world, which consists of thoughts, which are the property not only of human minds but at an elementary level of animal minds also. If these two worlds existed independently of one another, we might say that being manifests itself in two forms, matter and mind, and the problem we are considering would not exist. But mind and matter do not exist independently of one another: they interact every moment of the day. A simple instance of mind acting upon matter is the (mental) decision to raise one's arm producing the (physical) action corresponding to the decision. A simple example of matter acting on mind is the (physical) intake of alcohol producing the (mental) condition of drunkenness. Moreover, mind and matter seem to be so intimately associated that thought appears to be impossible except when there exists a physical brain to "produce" it. The problem, therefore, is: how are mind and matter related?

There are three possible answers: i that matter and mind do interact, ii that they do not interact but only seem to, and iii that either matter is a product of mind or mind a product of matter.

The most obvious answer is that what appears to happen actually does happen: that the mental world impinges upon the physical and vice versa. The difficulty about this answer is that the mental and material worlds seem to have no common factor. Thoughts appear to be totally immaterial and to be in no sense a form of energy. It is hard therefore to understand or even imagine how they can make a physical impact upon matter. Certainly, we cannot *see* them doing so, for, of course, we cannot see thoughts or apprehend them with any of our senses. The "obvious" answer is, in fact, no answer at all.

The second theory is that mind and matter only *seem* to interact but in reality do not do so. The plausibility of this solution lies in the apparent impossibility of any commerce between mind and matter. Its difficulty lies in the consequence which inevitably follows if they do not interact: namely, that mental and physical events occur independently but simultaneously. It is as if two clocks, A and B, stood side-by-side, both keeping perfect time. When clock A reads 12 o'clock, clock B chimes 12 times. It might seem as if clock A had caused clock B to chime, but this is not so. Both are keeping time independently. This solution, applied to the real world, seems fantastic, but the fact that many of the finest philosophical minds have considered it the most plausible explanation of the observed events is a measure of the philosophical difficulty of the mind-matter problem.

The two solutions just considered suppose that the apparent duality of mind and matter is a real duality: that mind and matter both exist, and exist independently. The third theory suggests that this duality is illusory, and that everything is matter or everything is mind. The view that everything is material is called materialism, and its basis is the supposition that thought is a product of matter and essentially physical. The view that matter is a product of thought is called idealism, and its basis is the supposition that "everything is in the mind" and that nothing exists which is not perceived: "esse est percipi"—to be is to be perceived—sums up this view. We shall encounter both theories in our discussion of the history of philosophy. Their extremism may seem startling, but it is really no more than another witness to the extreme difficulty of the problem.

4

THE BASIC metaphysical problem concerning man himself—as distinct from man as part of the universe as a whole—is whether he is free. There exists much evidence to show that man is not free, but that his actions and thoughts are determined by a very large number of influences which operate upon him from the moment he is born, and even before that moment. What a man is, is determined by his environment, the character of his parents—or the fact that he has no parents if his parents die while he is very young—the character of his ancestors, the behaviour of other people, the physical condition of his body and brain, and so on. Or—and this is the crux of the problem—is what a man is determined by these forces only to a degree? Is there a core of free will which enables a man to decide of his own volition what he shall be and what he shall do? The evidence for the existence of this core of free will is slight—yet in all societies men act as if every adult citizen were responsible for his actions. If he breaks the law he is punished, and this punishment is considered just—but our notions of justice would not be satisfied if man were actually no more responsible for his actions than, say, a tree is.

This is the metaphysical, and also the practical, problem of free will and determinism: it is another example of the apparent existence of two mutually-incompatible features of the world. No other metaphysical subject is so obviously of importance to the individual human being and no other arouses so much heated feeling in disputants. The hostility which still meets modern psychology is rooted in its tendency to provide evidence for determinism, for people desire very strongly to feel themselves free. (Why this desire should exist in a world in which human actions were completely determined is another riddle.) On the other hand, the violent animosity with which the philosophical movement called existentialism was met when it became prominent after the Second World War probably gained much of its force from the existentialists' assertion that mankind was entirely and limitlessly free, for the responsibility which total freedom brings with it is hard to face, especially if this freedom (if it is a reality) has not been used to achieve anything admirable.

The two extreme theories in this field—i that man is absolutely determined, ii that man is absolutely free—have so far encountered grave difficulties and objections. The determinist soon finds his determinism an insuperable handicap in dealing with any of the issues which seem to him of importance in human affairs. The Stoics, for example, taught that the course of a man's life was determined from the moment he was born, but also that men ought to adopt a certain ethical system (i.e. Stoicism). But it is self-contradictory to urge men to change their lives if their lives are absolutely determined from birth. The advocate of free will, on the other hand, finds no difficulty in preaching morals or in blaming and punishing those he considers immoral, but he has against him the impressive accumulation of evidence in favour of at least some degree of determinism. He must then, if he is honest, try to decide to what degree a particular action is wilful and to what degree determined and so beyond the control of the person performing it. And to reach this decision is—to put it no higher—hard. If the two extremes are difficult to maintain, it is just as difficult to maintain any position between them.

5

WHEN WE wish to describe a thing we enumerate its predicates:
we say that it is of a certain relative size, of a certain colour, of
a certain degree of hardness, of a certain shape, and so on. So
far as we know, everything that exists differs from everything
else that exists in all these respects: no two things are of the
same size, the same colour, the same degree of hardness, the
same shape. But one thing they do have in common: they all
exist. Existence is therefore not a predicate: it is no part of the
description of a thing to say that it exists, since to describe is to
differentiate, and existence is common to all existing things.
But if existence is not a predicate, what does it mean when we
say of a thing that it exists?

We here open up what is perhaps the ultimate question considered by philosophy: the question of the nature of being.
"Being" may be defined as "that which is"—not a very
satisfactory or enlightening definition, but it seems that we can
say no more about "being" than that it is. Its opposite is non-
being, or nothingness, and about nothingness we can say
nothing at all. Yet immediately we establish in our minds the
antithesis "being—nothingness", meaningful questions occur to
us. Is it possible to describe "being-as-such"—that is, being as
it is when we have taken away all the predicates of visibly-
existing objects? What is it which all things have in common
and which we give the name being, and which, since being is
everywhere, we ought to be able to recognise? Why is there
being at all, and not rather nothing? These questions and others
about the nature of being and existence-in-itself form the
department of metaphysics called ontology (from a part of the
Greek verb "to be").

The problem of the nature of God is best expressed for
philosophical purposes in terms of the problem of being. The
word "God" cannot be defined in a way that satisfies all uses of
it, whereas "being" can be adequately defined. Moreover, many
of the uses of the word "God" imply more than what might be
called "the ground of existence", which is the entity with

which ontology proposes to deal. For example, the word often
bears an ethical significance, so that the idea of moral goodness
is inherent in it, in which case it carries a predicate and the
subject-matter of ontology is, by definition, that which is
without predicates.

6

THE FOUR metaphysical problems we have looked at—those of
permanence and change, mind and matter, free will and determinism and the nature of being—are those which have
provided the subject-matter for most metaphysical systems. A
metaphysical system is a systematic effort to resolve these
problems by producing a comprehensive picture of the world.
The philosopher who ventures to do this makes the largest
claim for his abilities and performance it is possible to make,
and it is not surprising that he is usually met by a correspond-
ingly large scepticism. Such systems attract criticism and
usually succumb to it. And there have therefore been metaphysicians who have doubted, not the validity of this or that
metaphysical system, but the validity of metaphysics as such,
or the validity of metaphysical problems as posed. Critical
metaphysics is therefore a branch of the subject which treats of
the limits of metaphysical speculation and is concerned to
show the boundaries of meaningfulness in the posing of
questions. Systematic and critical metaphysics are equally
important parts of this department of philosophy.

There is a way around metaphysics and it is called phenomenalism—the thesis that all objects of knowledge are phenomena. Phenomenalism does not avoid the metaphysical
problems we have been discussing, nor does it judge them
insoluble or meaningless—it renders them irrelevant and thus
gets past them. You may think that, if it really does do this,
phenomenalism has a lot to be said for it.

Philosophically speaking, a "phenomenon" is anything which
is an object of perception or experience; metaphysics, being
the study of those things which transcend experience, divides

reality into phenomenon and that which is not phenomenon; "phenomenalism" is the assertion that this division is impermissible, that the subject matter of metaphysics is also phenomenon. If this assertion is accepted, many of the age-old problems of metaphysics disappear. Consider the question of "appearance and reality". Appearance is all that is phenomenon, reality is the non-phenomenal ("noumenal") substratum of which all phenomena are the appearance; but if it be asserted that everything of which we are aware must be phenomenon —if our being aware of it makes it phenomenon—then the idea of "appearance and reality" is also phenomenon and "reality" itself phenomenon, i.e. appearance: the distinction between phenomenal appearance and noumenal reality cannot be made. Consider the question of "freewill and determinism". The phenomena involved in this issue are sensations associated with actions: whether any or all of my actions are "free", or whether none of them is, is a problem beyond my capacity to solve, since I have no data other than the above-mentioned phenomena of sensation—I have no way of knowing whether the sensation of "freedom of will" is a product of free will or a consequence of the completest determinism. The distinction "free or determined" is thus also one I cannot make. In general: the distinction between what seems to be the case and what really is the case is abolished, and all phenomena are declared to be of equal validity. In place of this metaphysical distinction, and the search for "reality" from which it arose, phenomenalism introduces *comparison of phenomena*.

Ethics

WHEN MAN wishes to distinguish himself from, and elevate himself above, the rest of creation, he usually does so by claiming, not that he is stronger or more clever or in a vague way "better" than any other creature, but that only he possesses a moral sense. This distinction alone seems to him fundamental. Mankind knows good and evil or—a weakened form of this—right and wrong, and the animals do not. Only mankind is capable of goodness and wickedness. But goodness and wickedness cannot exist in an abstract form, only in the form of good and wicked actions. Certain acts are called good, certain acts wicked. Once this is understood, morality becomes a problem, and for two reasons. Firstly, it seems that if we are to call an act "good" we must be in possession of some criterion of "goodness", and we are then faced with the problem of accounting for this criterion—where does it come from? and how do we know it is valid? (And what do we mean by a "valid" criterion of goodness?). Secondly, we discover that there have been and still are differences of opinion as to what acts are good, and we are then faced with the problem of how to decide between differing moral opinions. The "moral sense" of man turns out to be no simple thing—indeed, we begin to doubt whether it has any real existence. Perhaps "morality" is an invention of ingenious man as a means to some—necessarily non-moral—end. These questions, of undoubted importance in human life, are among those considered in the department of philosophy called ethics, which may be defined as the theory of moral valuation.

This single term "ethics" is in ordinary speech used to denote what is in reality three branches of study. In modern work in this field these three branches are distinguished as follows: i morals or normative ethics, ii descriptive ethics, iii theoretical ethics or meta-ethics. We shall consider each of these in turn.

2

WHAT THE "plain man" usually means by "ethics" should, in philosophical speech, be termed "morals" or "normative ethics". The question considered under this heading is: "What is good?" or "What is right?" The answer may take the form of a general prescriptive statement or of "advice" on a particular issue, but it will in any case be an expression of moral opinion. The kind of problem involved is too obvious to require much illustration: "Is it right to kill in any circumstances?" is an example. The answer will be a statement of moral opinion, supported as a rule by argument. The philosophical difficulties in this field are also sufficiently obvious. They originate in the notorious elusiveness of moral considerations once we begin to present arguments in favour of a moral opinion, the problem being to find arguments that are themselves moral. For example, if I maintain that it is wrong to tell lies, and give as my reason for holding this moral opinion the view that civilised life requires that we should be able in general to rely on the word of others, I am giving a non-moral reason; for the endurance of civilised life is not obviously desirable on *moral* grounds. Or, if I should argue that civilisation is morally desirable, I should then have to say why I held *this* moral opinion, and I should have to speak of the benefits of civilisation in the form of security, health and longer life, the possibility of culture and learning, and so on: and none of these benefits is obviously desirable on *moral* grounds. Ultimately I might be driven to relying on a purely personal preference: "I prefer civilised life to the life of a savage", and then all pretence of morality would be gone. But it is not necessary to go to this extreme to realise that many ostensibly "good" actions cannot be fully justified on moral grounds, but only (if at all) on other grounds, for example on grounds of taste.

Western philosophy has been morally orientated from the outset: the earliest philosophers believed that the world possessed ethical significance—that good and evil were inherent in the heart and nature of things. And it has been this ethical component which has made it possible to claim for philosophy a place at the apex of human endeavour. Yet, as a branch of philosophy, that is to say as an object of rational investigation, "morality" poses the peculiar difficulty that it is not rational and that the search for a "rational ground of morality" is almost certainly a vain one: indeed, the absence of "reasons" is the most obvious fact about morality—moral commands are categorical, and one obeys them, not from intellectual assent, but out of a feeling of compulsion. Ask yourself why you think a certain kind of behaviour morally wrong and you will have to conclude that you do not "think" it wrong, you *feel* it to be so; ask yourself whether you have ever been argued into thinking something morally wrong (as opposed to inexpedient, foolish, dangerous, wasteful, unhealthy) and you will find that you could no more imagine such a thing than you could imagine being argued into finding something unpleasant: moral judgment and taste seem to have more in common with one another than either has with such considerations as expediency or reasonableness. It does seem that that which we recognise as a moral command is not grounded in anything else moral but itself constitutes morality—that moral conclusions never derive from moral premises but from premises which are non-moral. It is, for example, not hard to see how a desire for self-preservation could give rise to a morality in which killing is prohibited, or how a race in which the number of men and women is approximately equal will find it morally wrong for a man to have more than one wife or a woman more than one husband at one time: it may be harder to grasp that these moral commands *are* morality, that killing and polygamy are not wrong in themselves because nothing is wrong in itself, the concept "wrong in itself" being without content.

These considerations give rise to the further question whether "morals" can ever be a private matter—whether to speak of one's "personal convictions" in a moral sense can ever be other than a species of self-delusion. Morality, as we have been describing it, is a social phenomenon: it is a race, a nation, a caste, a group of some kind which decides what is good and evil, and does so in the interest of the group and not in that of the individuals which comprise it. That this is so emerges clearly in those cases in which morality coincides with law: in the case, for instance, of murder. If I shoot down a fellow citizen in the street and am put on trial for this offence against the law, it will be of no use for me to plead that I am "privately convinced" that shooting people is good, or that I am so constituted as to have a need to kill in the street. So far as morality is concerned my personal convictions and private feelings are beside the point, because morality is social and public, not private and personal.

The question "What is good?" is thus in all likelihood one that can be answered not in a prescriptive but only in a descriptive sense: the search for the nature of morality resolves itself into a comparison of moralities—into a phenomenalism of morals.

3

DESCRIPTIVE ETHICS is concerned, not with propounding morals, but with describing actually existing morals. That is, with answering the question: "What do people think or say is right?" The answer will be a statement of fact, not an expression of moral opinion. It is important that this branch should not be confused with morals or normative ethics, but confusion often occurs. For example, an account of Christian morality, which is an exercise in descriptive ethics, may pose as an exercise in normative ethics. The statement that this or that moral opinion is held by Christians may be offered as if it were an argument in favour of this opinion, whereas examination of the statement may reveal that no argument of this kind is in fact presented. "Preaching" in the ordinary meaning of the word is usually a descriptive-ethical address—"This is what

Christians believe"—posing (through unconscious confusion) as a normative-ethical address. It seems as if the speaker were giving grounds for holding certain moral opinions, whereas he is really stating moral opinions without giving grounds for them.

The objective of descriptive ethics is the discovery of the nature of morality—what morality really is. Just as a word means what most people think and say it means, so "what is right" is what most people think and say is right, and the task of descriptive ethics is to record what this is; what most people think and say is right has differed at different times, and differs in different places, and in recording these differences descriptive ethics evolves into comparative ethics; and comparative ethics, by recording different moral opinions, can reveal not only their differences but also what they have in common—what it is that makes them morality. If you and I differ over the value of the symphonies of Bruckner, this difference of opinion is clearly of a kind different from a difference we may have over the value of torture as a means of obtaining information: in the former case our aesthetic judgments differ, in the latter our ethical judgments, and in differentiating between them we advance nearer to a definition of an ethical judgment—nearer, that is, to a knowledge of what makes moral opinions moral.

4

FUNDAMENTAL TO any expression of moral opinion or description of ethical attitudes is an understanding of the meaning of moral terms. Theoretical ethics is concerned with the question: "What do moral terms mean?" The kind of question asked is: "When people say it is right to love one's neighbour, what does 'right' mean?" The answer will be a definition of the word "right", and will not involve an expression of moral opinion. This branch of ethics might be considered a part of epistemology in so far as it is concerned with the distinctions between moral knowledge and other kinds of knowledge. For example, the two statements "This wall is white" and "This action is wrong" appear to be in the same form and to belong to the same class of statement: they are both simple subject-predicate sentences. But the relation between subject and predicate in these sentences, although identical grammatically, is not identical epistemologically. We cannot be said to know that this action is wrong in the same sense as we know that this wall is white. In the case of the wall, our knowledge is empirical, that is, derived from observation. But in the case of the action, our knowledge is not empirical. What kind of knowledge is it, then? The answer could be that it is moral knowledge, which leaves us with the problem of the nature and origins of moral knowledge. A means to understanding what moral knowledge is lies in accurate definition of moral terms.

The three branches of ethics may be tabulated as follows:

i   *Normative ethics* (or morals) is concerned with the question "What is right?" and seeks to provide a rational basis for moral opinions.

ii *Descriptive ethics* is concerned with the question "What do people think or say is right?" and seeks to provide an account of actual moral opinions.

iii *Theoretical ethics* (or meta-ethics) is concerned with the question "When people say a thing is right, what does the word 'right' mean?" and seeks to provide a definition of moral terms.

THIS BRANCH of philosophy is concerned with the faculty for making aesthetic judgments, that is, judgments that some phenomenon of nature or art is beautiful, ugly, sublime, and so on. We continually make these judgments and argue about them, and aesthetics consists of reflections upon these judgments and upon the terms we employ when expressing them. It may be defined as the theory of the beautiful and of the faculty of taste.

On the most basic level, aesthetics is concerned to discover why beauty is beautiful and ugliness ugly. There cannot be the least doubt that it is the capacity to respond to the world aesthetically which for most people makes life worthwhile: a world we merely saw, heard and touched, but towards which we felt no kind of partiality, which we neither liked nor disliked, which neither pleased nor displeased us—a world, in short, towards which we failed to respond aesthetically—would be boring to a literally unimaginable degree. Possession of the "aesthetic sense" guarantees pleasure in living, and therefore life itself. We perceive something—a sight, a sound, a smell, a taste, a tactile sensation—and we are not indifferent to it; the great majority of such perceptions pass us by, we ignore them, we hardly notice them at all, but *this* one engages our attention, and we either seize and hold on to it or violently repulse and reject it: and we say of it that it is beautiful or ugly. What is it in us that does this? What does it mean that one thing is beautiful, another ugly, a third thing neither beautiful nor ugly but a matter of indifference to us? Are beauty and ugliness out there in the world, waiting to be discovered, and is recognition of them by the aesthetic sense analogous to the acquisition of knowledge, or do we ourselves bestow beauty and ugliness upon things which are in themselves aesthetically neutral? What are the conditions under which beauty and ugliness appear—what makes them appear? What makes a sound "musical"? Such questions as these provide the subject matter of aesthetics as "theory of the beautiful".

Aesthetics is also, of course, concerned with understanding the meaning and purpose of art. This undertaking resolves itself into the consideration of three different problems, and the student would do well to keep them distinct in his mind.

Firstly, there is the question "why art at all?" When "the artist" performs the activity which entitles him to this description, what is he really doing?—for art is, of course, first of all an activity, and only subsequently something that exists and is enjoyed. The reason for the activity "art" is what aesthetics must first seek when it investigates this realm of phenomena.

Then, secondly, it must consider art as "the creation of the beautiful". Given that beauty exists, either as a fact in the outside world or as a human mode of perception, how is its creation possible? What are the conditions under which a human artifact can arouse in us an aesthetic response? Why is this tune beautiful, that banal or unpleasing, when they differ from one another in so few respects? Why does one arrangement of lines and colours give a feeling of satisfaction, another fail to do so?

Thirdly, aesthetics must seek to explain art as "transfiguration of the ugly"—ugly here understood as meaning all that is unpleasing or dreadful in life. The grand example in this realm is of course tragedy, in which the worst aspects of existence are, through an aesthetic operation, made not merely enjoyable but the most profoundly enjoyable of all artistic experiences. Aesthetics has to try to explain *King Lear*.

Applied Philosophy

THE APPLICATION of philosophical ideas and methods to other branches of study may be called applied philosophy. It is reasonable to speak of a "philosophy of" anything to which reasoned argument is applied: for example, one may speak of "philosophy of education", meaning a theory of educational methods and aims founded on philosophical principles. Four such applications are of particular importance.

The application of philosophy to religious questions comes near to theology on one hand and to metaphysics on the other. It differs from both, however, in being essentially an attempt to explain religious concepts in philosophical terms and to decide which of such concepts are rational. Its concern with philosophical terms and arguments marks it off from theology, its concern with religion marks it off from metaphysics.

To philosophy of religion belongs the examination of the ideas of God which exist or have existed, together with their feasibility, and of the arguments for the existence of God.

Behind the recording of past events and the writing of history stands the question: "What is the nature of history?" Is it, for example, a series of events related only chronologically, that is, merely following one upon the other in time, or can some ordering principle be discovered to underlie the procession of events? Can we learn from the past anything about the future? Does history repeat itself, and if it does, in what way? These and similar questions are the concern of philosophy of history.

Another type of historical question which is essentially philosophical is the problem of the value of historical study: whether the amassing of facts about the past is valuable in itself, or whether knowledge of the past is a means to some present or future end.

The application of philosophical methods to a study of law takes the form of an examination of the idea of justice, of the end which law should serve, of the nature of legality in its relation to good and evil, and all the problems connected with the ordering of the behaviour of men living together in society.

Since men live in a society of some kind, it is of vital importance to know what kind of society is most desirable. The kind of society we have depends upon the kind of government we have. Politics is the science and art of government, and political philosophy is the application of philosophical principles to the problems of government. Political philosophy discusses towards what ends government should strive and how these ends are to be achieved, and the character of actually operating political theories.

Part Two

Introduction to the History of Western Philosophy

Prefatory note. No one man has yet written a history of Western philosophy which has satisfied everyone, and perhaps the task is impossible. Certainly, nothing of the kind is attempted here. For the beginner, a detailed history would be indigestible : what he requires is an outline of the way in which philosophy has developed during the past 2,500 years or so, presented sufficiently briefly for him to grasp this development as a whole. The following introduction to the history of philosophy omits many well-known names, and no philosophy is presented in its entirety. What is presented is the grand sweep of philosophical speculation from the earliest times to the present day. The emphasis is upon exposition and criticism is kept to a minimum : the beginner must know what philosophical views have been held before he can attempt any critique. The narrative should be read almost as a story is read —except that there is no denouement : most of the major problems of philosophy are as open now as when speculation about them first began.

I   Greek Philosophy

I

THE EARLIEST philosophers were born in the Greek colonial cities of Asia Minor and southern Italy in the 6th century B.C. No century in the history of mankind was more momentous than this one. The world we know today is as it is because of what happend then. It was the century of Buddha, Confucius, Lao Tse and Isaiah, who created for mankind a true religious consciousness distinct from superstition arising from fear and, in the first three instances, free from belief in gods or God. It was the century of Cyrus, the founder of the Persian Empire, the first example of politics on a grand scale and the best organised political structure before the Roman Empire. It was also the century during which there emerged into history a new type of man, at first a hard-pressed tribe on the fringe of the great empire of the Middle East, later to make the whole world his empire and to compel mankind to accept him as its norm : Greek man, *European* man. The Greeks were the first Europeans and what we now think of as distinctively European in modes of living and reacting towards the world, is what in the 6th century distinguished the Greeks from their neighbours. The Greeks were the first scientists, the first mathematicians and geometers, the first map-makers, the first historians, the first astronomers. Their originality was prodigious and in nothing were they more original than in their invention of rational thinking about the world and about themselves.

The word "philosophy" derives from the Greek words "philos", meaning "lover of" or "friend of", and "sophia", meaning "wisdom" or "knowledge". But the word "sophia" was applied beyond the borders of what we should now mean by philosophy and included the sciences, especially what we now call physics and astronomy, and the practical applications of these. Aristotle described the earliest philosophers—that is, those who came before Socrates—as "physiologoi", which means "investigators of nature" or students of "physis"— nature—as a whole. Of course, there had been "students of nature" before the pre-Socratic philosophers, and there were such students living in Greece and the rest of the ancient world contemporaneously with them. What entitles the men we are about to consider to the title of "philosopher" is that they abandoned the age-old *mythological* mode of interpretation of nature and pioneered the *description* of nature in rational terms. What distinguished them from the astrologers and other "sages" of their time was that they believed the world could be understood by reason and described in terms of natural phenomena and not, as hitherto, in terms of myths. It will be grasped at once that this step was an indispensable precondition for the development of science in any form and for the control of natural forces. So long as nature was conceived of as a divine realm and natural phenomena as the operations of gods, the world remained incomprehensible and uncontrollable and rational science an impossibility. What in Babylon and Egypt looks like science—the prediction of eclipses, for instance—is no more than accidental discovery: that eclipses could be predicted was known, but why they could be predicted and how they were caused was still a mystery.

2

THE PRE-SOCRATIC philosophers—the line from Thales to Democritus—present us with a remarkably steady and consistent development: they follow one another not only in time but also logically, and this is because each was concerned fundamentally with the same problem—the nature of reality —and knew the work of his predecessors. Our own knowledge of their work derives from fragmentary remains of their writings and from accounts by later writers, who had read what is now lost.

By common consent, the originator of philosophy and the first man of science was Thales, who lived in Miletus, a Cretan colony on the coast of Asia Minor, in the latter half of the 6th century B.C. He predicted an eclipse of the sun which occurred in 585 B.C. and was numbered by the Greeks among their "Seven Wise Men", although he probably owed this distinction more to his skill in practical affairs than for his philosophical speculation. Thales was the first man of whom we have record to attempt to describe the world rationally instead of mythologically, and his principal theory was that everything was fundamentally water. This hypothesis needs explaining if it is not to seem ridiculous. It rests upon the assumption that in the last resort the immense variety of observed nature may be reduced to a single fundamental substance or principle. In antique Greece, "nature" had been reduced to four "elements": earth, water, mist and fire. Air was regarded as a refined form of mist and the upper air—the hot, bright sky of the eastern

Mediterranean—as a more refined form still, the so-called "aether", and really a kind of fire. Earth was imagined as solidified water—a more deeply-frozen form of ice. Thales' proposition was that all these forms might be reduced to one basic form: water. It was, of course, a guess: neither Thales nor his successors had any way of verifying their hypotheses experimentally. But it must be remembered that all hypotheses are in some sense guesses: science proceeds by guesses which are confirmed or refuted by experiment. Thales' innovation is the scientific language in which his hypothesis is couched. The division of the world into what appears to be the case and what really is the case took place long before Thales, and may even be a consequence of thinking as such—of the fact that men are *and* think, and therefore believe there exists two worlds, one inhabited by the body, the other by the mind: the natural and the supernatural worlds, appearance and reality. In Thales, this fundamental belief receives materialist, scientific expression: "reality" is water, "appearance" is the diverse shapes into which water is transformed: and this alone suffices to make of Thales the inaugurator of science.

Thales' successor was Anaximander, also of Miletus, who flourished about 560 B.C. Anaximander was in agreement with Thales' proposition that unity must underly the plurality of nature but was struck by two objections to Thales' postulate that water was basic to all other elements. The world seemed to consist not so much of equivalent forms of one substance as of parallel opposites—wet and dry, hot and cold, for instance—and this seemed to exclude the idea that any of these opposites was basic. And since these opposites were incompatible with one another, if one were basic, it must have conquered the others. Thales, in fact, had overemphasised "wet", whereas it seemed to Anaximander more reasonable to suppose that both wet and dry emerged from a substance common to both. This substance could not be part of the developed world, so Anaximander called it "the Indefinite"—an undeveloped substance from which all the elements arose. To account for the continued existence of opposites with neither finally triumphant, he introduced the idea of "reparation", a kind of natural justice, through which every element was assigned bounds. When it overstepped these bounds it was compelled to make reparation to its opposite so as to preserve the balance of things.

Such a theory can be regarded as purely scientific, concerned only with explaining why the physical world is as it is: but many have recognised in it an ethical component, a statement not only of what is but also of what ought to be. "The beginning and origin of the things that are", Anaximander says, "is the Indefinite [*apeiron*]. Into that from which the things that are arise, however, they pass away again, as they are obliged to do; for they give satisfaction and reparation to one another for their injustice, as is appointed according to the ordering of time". These sentences, the earliest surviving complete sentences of Western philosophy, contain, it has been suggested, the ethical judgment that all created things deserve the destruction which is awaiting them, and that Anaximander is thus an ethical pessimist of a kind similar to Schopenhauer.

Anaximander also believed in the existence of many worlds other than our own, and that the earth was not fixed in space. He likewise understood that in the cosmos there is no absolute up and down but that every world has its own up (away from it) and down (towards it).

The third of the Milesian philosophers, Anaximenes, is of less importance than Thales or Anaximander. He flourished about 545 B.C. and, neglecting Anaximander's conception of "the Indefinite", returned to Thales' idea of a single developed element as the basis of the others, but chose, instead of water, mist, and attributed the metamorphoses of mist to degrees of concentration: fire, he said, was mist rarified, water and earth mist condensed. The originality of this concept lies in the suggestion of some *means* by which one element could change into other elements: by being more or less concentrated. Anaximenes believed that mist was to the world what the soul was to man: its source of life.

The scientific rationalism of Miletus in the east of the Greek world was matched by the development of philosophical mysticism in the west, and the contrast is made very vivid by the quite matter-of-fact rationality of Xenophanes of Colophon, who flourished at the turn of the 6th-5th centuries and was greatly influenced by the scientific bias of Miletus. Xenophanes is not of the first rank as a philosopher, but he is striking as an example of the critical detachment possible to an educated Greek in this era. He is best known for his total scepticism concerning religion. He found the Olympian pantheon incredible, and remarked that if lions had gods they would give them the form of lions, that the Ethiopians' gods were black and snub-nosed. There is in fact, said Xenophanes, only one God, and he in no way resembles man. It follows that he cannot be defined, although one can believe that "life" is the thought of this one God. Xenophanes was also a complete sceptic concerning the possibility of knowledge: the facts of nature were beyond the reach of mind, he thought, and if a man happened to express a truth about them, this was an accident and he could have no way of knowing that it *was* the truth. Xenophanes seems to have liberated himself completely from the mythological mode of thought. He no longer views all things in terms of human qualities—the characteristic error of nature mythology. And he lacks all respect for tradition. He is the kind of "free spirit" whose existence is an essential precondition of the development of unhampered philosophical speculation.

The western mystical tradition was founded by Pythagoras of Samos, who flourished about 530 B.C. and established a community of disciples at Croton, in southern Italy. Bertrand Russell says of him: "I do not know of any other man who has been as influential as he was in the sphere of thought", and the source of this influence lay in the inferences Pythagoras drew from the facts of mathematics, of which he was the inventor. The union of mathematics and mysticism is not one which seems obvious to a modern mind, but it is not difficult to see how Pythagoras came to draw mystical conclusions from numbers. (It should be remarked that Pythagoras' followers attributed all their doctrine to "the Master", and it is no longer possible to say how much of "Pythagoreanism" originated in the mind of Pythagoras himself and how much in the minds of his disciples.) We must imagine Pythagoras as having had a sudden insight into the possibilities of mathematical demonstration and objectifying his delight as a theory of life. That $2+2=4$ is a piece of exact knowledge derived not from observation but "analytically"—the conclusion follows from the definition of "2". (This principle is more obviously true in the case of such a number as "-2", which corresponds to nothing observable). This suggests that "truth" may be arrived at by pure thinking, divorced from observation and experiment, and that because the "truths" of mathematics are exact, they are in some way of a higher kind than the "facts" derived from observation. Pythagoras was therefore the originator of rationalism in the philosophic sense of the word; that is, of the idea that philosophic truth may be arrived at by a process of pure thought. Mathematics seemed also to offer a science of "ideal" objects—objects existing in thought and not in the objective world—and this gave rise to the belief in the existence of an entire supra-sensible world of "ideal" objects, superior in their purity to the objects of the mundane world. And further, that it is possible to have exact knowledge of the supra-sensible world. Thus the central tenets of Plato and those who followed him can be traced back to Pythagoras and his mystique of mathematics.

Pythagoras discovered that the basis of the musical scale is numerical; that is, that harmonic intervals can be explained in terms of numerical ratios; and his followers extended this discovery to saying that the basis of the world was numerical. They thought of simple numbers as forming shapes, as on dice, and they imagined that objects were formed by configurations of these spatial numbers.

Pythagoreanism also involved belief in the transmigration of souls and embodied a large number of tabu prohibitions—but the mathematically-minded separated themselves from disciples who took this part of the doctrine seriously. As a whole, Pythagoreanism seems a fanciful blend of insight and nonsense, and there are some confusions in the doctrine which suggests very strongly that it was never propounded as a whole by Pythagoras or any other single individual. The distinction between a mystical, quasi-religious movement and a self-consistent metaphysic emerges clearly when we consider the first metaphysical system to be devised by a single philosopher: the system of Heraclitus.

A struggle between opposites which produces unceasing change is the basis of the metaphysic of Heraclitus, who was born in Ephesus and flourished about 500 B.C. Fire is Heraclitus' basic substance: "This world," he says, "which is the same for all things, was not created by one of the gods nor by any man, but was and is and always will be an ever-living fire, kindled by measure and extinguished by measure". As with Anaximander, the eternal conflict is perpetuated by cosmic justice, which prevents the victory of any one of the warring parties. This struggle, which never ceases and which can have no outcome, is the only sort of permanence there is: nothing is fixed, everything is in flux. "One cannot step into the same river twice," says Heraclitus, and this he intends as an image of the continual flux of reality. What appears as unity and permanence is actually the momentary uniting of opposites before breaking loose again. All this sounds quite modern, suggesting as it does something of Hegel and Nietzsche and the modern dynamic view of material substance, and it introduces us to the problem of permanence and change, or, in other terms, being and becoming.

Permanent existence—"being"—and constant change—"becoming"—both seem to characterise the world as we know it, yet both cannot be fundamental. If being is fundamental then becoming is illusory, if becoming is fundamental then being is illusory. Heraclitus opted for becoming, and maintained that reality was constantly changing, the agent of change being conflict between opposites. Being, he thought, was a fiction, an illusion of the mind. He was followed, chronologically, by a philosopher who thought just the reverse, namely that change was impossible and being the only reality. This notion, which sounds strange to modern ears, was one of the most fruitful concepts of early philosophy and led directly to the atomic theory and thence, at a great remove, to modern atomic physics.

Born in Elea in southern Italy at the beginning of the 5th century B.C., Parmenides has been called the inventor of logic. Although he was hardly that—there had been logical argument before Parmenides—he was the first philosopher to base his philosophy on logical argument. Parmenides denied the logical possibility of change and motion and argued that the only logical possibility was unchanging being. We can, he said, speak only of what *is*, and not of what *is not*: this is the basis of his argument. Everything corresponding to a word must exist *now* —otherwise we could not speak of it. Therefore it cannot come into existence (have not been) or pass out of existence (cease to be). But "change" means having not been and then ceasing to be, and is therefore logically impossible. For a similar reason, motion is also impossible. For there to be motion there must be empty space in which and into which objects can move, but empty space—the void—is by definition nothing, and cannot exist. Therefore motion cannot exist. To describe change and motion, said Parmenides, involves describing that which is not, and this is logically impossible.

The sole logically-possible reality is a single, infinite and motionless being, which Parmenides called "the One", and the world of sense, which admits change and motion, is an illusion. This conflicts violently with actual experience, and to refute Parmenides and the Eleatic philosophy—the name, adopted by Parmenides' followers, derives from his birthplace—became a major preoccupation of pre-Socratic philosophy.

All the philosophers we have considered up to now shared the belief that the world must be reducible to unity, but in the Eleatic philosophy this belief seemed to have led to a patent absurdity, and the two philosophers we are now to consider sought to surmount this absurdity by abandoning belief in ultimate unity.

Empedocles, who was born at Acragas in Sicily and flourished about 450 B.C., is, next to Pythagoras, the most notable representative of the scientific-mystic combination characteristic of the western extremity of the Greek world which contrasts with the materialism and practical science of Miletus in the Eastern extremity. He is credited with having discovered that air is a corporeal substance, and he maintained that the four elements earth, water, fire and air were distinct and different, not forms of one single substance. These elements he called the "roots" of material life. All other substances, he asserted, were produced by the combination of these roots in varying proportions; and this combining and separating appeared as "change". The elements were impelled to combine by "love" and driven apart again by "strife"—love and strife also being material elements.

Anaxagoras, who was born at Clazomene in Ionia and flourished about 450 B.C., taught that each of the four elements is present in all material substance and that any particular substance appears to be what it contains most of. Thus, for instance, air also contains earth, fire and water, but in small quantity compared with the quantity of air: it therefore appears to be entirely air. All matter is infinitely divisible, but even the smallest particle contains all the elements. The "life-force" which informs the world of matter and is its source of energy Anaxagoras called "mind" (*nous*).

These two theories were evolved in an attempt to reconcile the permanent and the changing features of the world; in terms of rival philosophies, to reconcile Heraclitus (everything changes) and Parmenides (nothing changes), both of which extremes seemed to contradict actual experience. But they are obviously unsatisfactory, and the theory which was to provide the concept by which the changing and the unchanging might actually be reconciled is the one we are now to consider.

The atomic theory originated with Leucippus, was elaborated by Democritus, revived by Epicurus, and was the subject of one of the greatest Latin poems, "De Rerum Natura" of Lucretius. As an account of reality it represents a great advance upon anything attempted previously, and it can best be understood as an answer to the dilemma created by Parmenides.

According to the theory of atoms, the world consists of two

parts: matter and the void. Parmenides had maintained that the void was by definition nothing and therefore could not exist, but the atomists asserted that it did exist but was incorporeal. In order to exist, a thing need not have material substance. This is true and a complete answer to Parmenides' argument concerning the void. In addition to the void, the world consists of matter, and matter is composed of physically-indivisible atoms. Each atom is Parmenides' "One". Individual atoms are unchanging, but change consists in the formation and disruption of groups of atoms. Thus coming to be and ceasing to be are, as Parmenides maintained, impossible, for the atoms are immutable; what appears to be creation and dissolution is actually the grouping and regrouping of atoms, which possess solidity, shape, weight and size, but not colour, smell, taste or heat.

Upon this basis was erected a complete materialist explanation of the world. Coarse material was said to be composed of coarse atoms, fine material of fine atoms. The soul, which was associated with breath, was composed of very fine atoms, and sense perception involved the emission of atoms from the organs of sense. Thought was also explained materialistically as an emission of atoms.

The atomic theory was not a scientific hypothesis, for no means were available for verifying or refuting it. It was rather an inspired guess which made possible the development of science in the western world: it provided the *concept* of matter composed of atoms in various combinations without which the discovery of the actual physical nature of matter would hardly have occurred. The physicists of the 17th century who propounded the atomistic theory of matter did so under the direct influence of the atomists of antiquity, from whom they derived the atomic concept, and the 17th century theory led directly to modern atomic physics. Of almost equal influence was the distinction drawn between solidity, shape, weight and size (which atoms were said to possess) and colour, smell, taste and heat (which they were said not to possess). The former is a list of what were later to be called "primary" qualities, the latter of "secondary" qualities. To have distinguished these qualities one from another was a great advance and one that made the development of empirical science possible.

One further striking characteristic of Greek atomism is that it is the first mechanistic description of the world divorced from speculation about the purpose of the world: all trace of the mythological mode of thought has vanished.

The founder of atomism, Leucippus, was probably born in Abdera in the middle of the fifth century B.C., but he is a shadowy figure who cannot be clearly distinguished from his successor, Democritus, who was certainly born in Abdera and who flourished about 420 B.C. Democritus was a contemporary of Socrates and the last, and in some respects the most gifted, of the pre-Socratic philosophers. He was a mathematician of great brilliance and wrote on many subjects, including biology and music. His ethics are virtually those of Epicurus, and since Epicurus also adopted his atomism, Democritus must be considered the real founder of the very influential Epicurean philosophy.

By the time of Democritus, the study of philosophy was a recognised part of Greek education: the professional teachers of the subject were called sophists. The modern meaning of "sophist"—one who argues with quibbles and reasoning he knows to be false but hopes will deceive—must not be attached to the professional sophists of Greece, although it was the practice of many of them which led to the modern meaning of the word. The sophists taught rhetoric, dialectic (how to argue) and the various accomplishments necessary for social success. The best of them, such as Protagoras and Gorgias, were philosophers and in no way "sophists" in the modern sense. But because they were paid tutors and were expected to produce tangible results, however achieved, the common run of sophists gained the reputation for intellectual dishonesty or "sophistry". To the "plain man" of those times, any philosopher was a sophist simply because he taught philosophy. Socrates and Plato were known as sophists, although they were not members of that profession, and consequently mistrusted by the people of

Athens. It may be that the widespread suspicion of philosophers on the part of the unphilosophical which has been evident at all subsequent times had its origin in the often justified suspicions of the Athenians against the sophists. The profession disappeared in the fourth century B.C. with the setting-up of permanent universities.

Protagoras, who was born in Abdera and flourished about 450-440 B.C., was an accomplished philosopher of a very marked scepticism concerning religion and the possibility of real knowledge. He maintained that men could have no knowledge of the gods and could not know whether they existed or not: he was what would now be called an "agnostic". No absolute truths could be known, because the nature of each man entered into his judgments: this is the meaning of his famous saying: "Man is the measure of all things."

These men we have been considering, from Thales to Democritus and Protagoras, are among the noblest in the story of mankind, and before going on to the great Athenian age of Socrates, Plato and Aristotle, it will be worthwhile to consider what they were like as individuals. As might be expected, it is not easy to distinguish fact from legend, but even legend is informative, since it tell us of the impression these first philosophers made upon their contemporaries.

All are represented as being of a striking individuality amounting in some cases to eccentricity. All are capable of inspiring great devotion in their followers, even if, as in the case of Heraclitus, they disdain followers and speak in a deliberately obscure way. They are indifferent to success as usually understood, but aspire to success of a superior kind. None of them has any respect for the past, for tradition or for the gods, although they do not all make a point of this. Explicitly or implicitly they all repudiate Homer and the ancient ways and laugh at the tales of gods and heroes, whom they consider more or less ridiculous. Essentially, they all feel that what they have to offer—philosophy and science—is superior to the old tradition and the old religion and that their way of living is better than that of the admired Homeric heroes.

So much they have in common: but as individuals they are distinct, each with his own very pronounced characteristics. Thales was a man of affairs who took a prominent part in the life of his city but expected no material reward from philosophy. The story is told that, because he was able to predict an abundance of olives he made a corner in olive oil, thus proving that a scientist and philosopher could make a fortune if he wished but that he sought his reward elsewhere. This lesson was not lost on the Greeks who followed him, and impracticality was almost a watchword among the intellectual. Euclid, for example, when asked by a member of his audience what profit he gained from geometry, replied: "Give me a penny, then." Heraclitus presents a contrast to Thales. Although entitled by birth to a leading place in the government of Ephesus, he rejected not only it but the city as such with the utmost contempt and disappeared into the country. His loathing for his fellow citizens was almost pathological, yet he was greatly admired by those he despised. Of all the Greek philosophers he approaches most closely to the passionateness and intensity of a Hebrew prophet.

Heraclitus seemed to care little whether he was understood or not and he wrote in an oracular and aphoristic manner which disdained logical order. Parmenides, on the other hand, was so anxious to be understood that he has gained the reputation of being the first logician. This being so, it usually comes as a surprise to the student to learn that Parmenides presented his philosophy in a poem and not in a treatise. It would not have been surprising to his contemporaries, to whom it would have seemed a perfectly natural way in which to express one's thoughts.

Pythagoras and Empedocles were mystics who mingled things which now seem to have no common factor: in the case of Pythagoras it was mysticism and mathematics, in the case of Empedocles mysticism and medicine. Both seem to have had something of the crank and the quack in their make-up, and Empedocles especially was a poseur and mystificator. The most revealing legend about Empedocles is that he died by leaping into the crater of Mount Etna under the impression he would not perish but somehow survive. One cannot imagine such a tale repeated of Thales or Heraclitus—who is supposed to have thrown himself on to a dunghill in a mood of utter misanthropy and expired of contempt. Almost nothing is known of the life of Pythagoras, which is a pity, because he is the one pre-Socratic philosopher about whom we should like to know everything. He was certainly a genius of a very high order, indeed one of the most original of all minds. To get his measure, we should have to be able to compare him with Newton and Einstein.

Anaxagoras, Democritus and Protagoras belong to the earliest fully-historical age of Greece, the age in which Athens first enters the story of philosophy. Early Greek philosophy was not Athenian and later Greek philosophy was produced by men who were not Athenians. But the influence of Athens on philosophy was immense, chiefly because, of the three greatest philosophers of ancient times, two *were* Athenian and the third learned philosophy from them. The subject was brought to Athens by Anaxagoras and took firm root. It is not too much to say that philosophy became a passion among the ruling class of Athens. But it was a man of the people, Socrates, who was the first Athenian philosopher, and who decisively changed the course of philosophy.

Philosophers hitherto had been insatiable for knowledge and had applied themselves to all manner of problems and puzzles, practical as well as theoretical. They had been on the whole extroverted and eager to explain the phenomena of the world visible to all men. They concerned themselves little with private ethics or abstract thought. They were in touch with the solid world, however strange they sometimes made it appear. With Socrates, philosophy took a new direction. His revolution was to introduce private ethics into philosophy and to give it a central place, and to emphasise dialectics and abstract argument. This meant turning inward, away from the universe and towards man and oneself.

3

THE LIFE of Socrates is known to us chiefly from the works of his pupil Plato. There is no good reason for thinking that the figure presented there does not correspond, broadly speaking, with the real man (although we can be fairly certain that Plato sometimes attributes to his master ideas which were really Plato's). Socrates was born in Athens in 469 B.C. and lived there until, in 399 B.C., he was put to death after being convicted of "corrupting the young men and not believing in the gods of the city". The charge was almost certainly political in essence, and, if Plato's account of the trial is accurate, Socrates' defence, which was essentially a defence of the right to free speculation, was couched in terms calculated to anger rather than appease his judges. After he had been condemned, Socrates refused all forms of assistance in escaping—which, one understands, would have been fairly easy—and insisted on waiting for the day of his execution and then drinking poison, as the law prescribed. Socrates' bearing during his last days, as described by Plato, challenges comparison with that of Jesus as described in the Gospels, and has made him the symbolic representative of *self-control through reason*. It is as the champion of reason and the teacher of how to live and to face death in the light of rationality that Socrates is a figure of world-historical significance. A brief account cannot do him justice, and fortunately one is not needed: Plato is one of the world's great literary artists and his account of Socrates' life and death, especially the *Apology of Socrates*, the *Crito* and the *Phaedo*, are perhaps the first original philosophical texts the beginner should attempt.

How far Socrates' opinions as presented by Plato are those of the real man, it is impossible to say. Socrates wrote no books, but taught orally, by means of question and answer. The discussions which supposedly resulted are the subject-matter of Plato's dialogues. It seems certain that, whatever detailed opinions Plato may have put into the mouth of Socrates, he is historically accurate in representing him as being concerned primarily with ethics and the nature of virtue, as seeking for universal definitions (what this means will be explained shortly) and as conducting discussions by means of dialectic, framing syllogisms and relying upon demonstrative proofs. There is no need to go further than this in the present context.

4

PLATO IS the first philosopher in the full meaning of the word, and one of the two most influential thinkers in history (the other being his pupil Aristotle). He was born in Athens about 427 B.C. of aristocratic parentage and died there in 347 B.C. During his 20s he came under the influence of Socrates and adopted philosophy as his life's work. After Socrates' execution in 399 B.C., Plato left Athens for a time, but he was back again by about 385 B.C., for by that date he had founded a "museum", or society of the muses, near the grove of Academus at Athens, for the discussion and teaching of philosophy. The "Academy", as it came to be called, was the first university. Its ultimate purpose was to improve political life by teaching good government and Plato's philosophy has the training of good rulers as its basic aim. For much of his remaining 40 years, he stayed in Athens, teaching at the Academy and writing his works. All his writings are extant and, taken together, constitute the most considerable achievement of any philosopher.

The study of Plato's philosophy is the most rewarding introduction to the subject the beginner can attempt. The first thing to note is that Plato is already the heir of a long tradition. From Pythagoras he derived the idea of a supra-sensible reality, the importance of mathematics and the sense of speaking to a small group of the elect. From Heraclitus he had the idea of continual change. From Parmenides he took the dichotomy between appearance and reality and the unreliability of the senses, and from Socrates the primacy of ethical problems and the problem of universals. This diversified inheritance leads in Plato to the first instance of a philosophy which seeks to combine the logical, epistemological and metaphysical aspects of philosophy on the one hand, with the ethical and aesthetic on the other. But an attempt to discover the nature of reality and an attempt to discover the nature of the good life are not obviously parts of the same discipline, and Plato's systematic combination of them into a single science—"philosophy" in the full sense— was responsible for very many of the difficulties which subsequent philosophers down to the present day have had to contend with. Among the pre-Socratics, the discovery of the nature of reality was an end in itself; but Socrates introduced the ethical question into philosophy and in Plato the discovery of the nature of reality is essentially only a preliminary to the discovery of the nature of the good life: and this is in turn, only a preliminary to the discovery of the nature of good govern- ment. But whether ethical questions can possibly be resolved in this manner is a problem fundamental to philosophy and one which was posed rather than answered by Plato. It may be that the attempt is wholly misguided and the notion that it is possible totally false. If so, Plato was the most formidable teacher of error in the world's history.

Aristotle tells us (in his *Metaphysics*) that Socrates sought to define universals, but did not seek to make the definitions exist apart; and since Plato does seek to make the definitions exist apart, we are perhaps justified in thinking that this is the point at which Plato's philosophy becomes original. The problem of universals has to do with the meaning of descriptive words. If we describe two animals as horses, we do so because both possess the characteristics of the animal we call "horse". But these two horses are not identical: they differ in height, weight, shape and colour and all their parts differ in those respects; no two horses are alike. It follows, therefore, that the definition of the word "horse" cannot define any individual, actually-exist- ing horse, since if it did so it would define that one animal alone and not all the other "horses" which differ from it. To what, then, does the word "horse" refer? It seems to refer to a kind of universal horse, an essential "horseness" which has no visibly concrete existence, but exists only in the mind and to which individual horses only approximate. The word "horse" is therefore a universal term and its definition a universal definition. We advance the problem a further step if we consider geometrical shapes, for example an equilateral triangle. We know that in reality there are no equilateral triangles, that if we attempt to draw one, we can produce only an approximation. Furthermore, all the equilateral triangles ever drawn differ not only from a perfect equilateral triangle, but also from one another. Yet the words "equilateral triangle" undoubtedly refer to something; therefore, what they refer to must be a kind of universal equilateral triangle existing nowhere in space but only in the mind.

Socrates sought to define universal terms such as these, and his inquiry into the nature of virtue was allied to this undertaking. For example, if we ask what is meant by "courage" it is not enough to point to a courageous man or to describe his actions. It seems that there must be a kind of universal "courage" of whose nature individual courageous acts partake.

It was upon this inquiry after universal definitions that Plato founded his theory of Forms (or Ideas). According to his theory, the universals exist apart: that is, one perfect horse exists in a supra-sensible reality, and individual horses are imperfect reflections of this perfect prototype. The one perfect horse alone is "real", its reflections being only "appearances". Similarly, there exists one perfect equilateral triangle, and it alone is real. The whole visible world is a reflection or "appearance" of a "real" world composed of perfect prototypes. These prototypes are the "Forms" of reality, and they can be apprehended, not through the senses, but only through the mind.

Universal terms are used constantly and have meaning, and it was only by supposing that they refer to the Forms that Plato could explain this fact.

Now, in a similar way Plato supposed that the virtues must be reflections of perfect Forms: there must exist a Form of courage, justice, and so on, of whose essence individual instances of courage and justice partake. Above all, there exists a Form of "the Good". The object of philosophical inquiry is to discover the nature of the Forms, and ultimately the nature of the Form of "the Good". He who does this will be not only wise but virtuous, since knowledge of the Good must lead man to perform the Good, it being impossible to act in a way contrary to what one conceives as good. From this it follows that evil is ignorance, and that the way to virtue and the way to knowledge are the same—that is, both will be attained through philosophy.

This doctrine may be called Plato's absolutism. He believes that there is one Good, which is the same for all men, that goodness is something not dependent on opinion or desire, but is, like mathematical truth, objective. That which is good is good absolutely, and remains good whether or not anyone knows it is good. From this moral absolutism follows his political authoritarianism, or as we should now say, totalitarianism.

Plato's political philosophy is expounded chiefly in his *Republic*, one of the longest and finest of his works and one of the most thrilling philosophical texts in existence. Opinions differ as to how the *Republic* ought to be read. If, as is generally believed, it is a detailed programme for an ideal state, it should be read as an exposition of totalitarianism in an extreme form, since the programme outlined involves the suppression of most of what we count as civil rights and civic liberty in favour of what Plato thinks is an ideal political constitution. The Athens of Plato's day was democratic and decaying, the Sparta of his day totalitarian and strong; this led him, it seems, to an initial bias in favour of authoritarian government which was greatly strengthened by his theory of perfect Forms, which made it easy for him to imagine that an ideal "Form" of state existed if only philosophers could discover what it was. But it is possible to read the work as an exposition, not of a programme for some actual state, but of the considerations which ought, in Plato's opinion, to underly the laws of *any* state. There are several passages in the *Republic* which suggest that Socrates, who is the expositor, does not believe the ideal state can exist on earth and that what he is offering is a prolegomenon to the making of laws. This suggestion is strengthened by the fact that when, in his later years, Plato attempts what is undoubtedly a programme for an ideal state (in the dialogue called the *Laws*), his programme consists of a list of legal provisions backed by legal argument, but includes no discussion of abstract justice. But however it is read, the *Republic* offers the sternest and most rewarding challenge to the believer in liberal institutions to justify his beliefs: if he does not like Plato's ideal state, he must be prepared to counter Plato's arguments in its favour.

The crux of Plato's political philosophy follows from his doctrine that there is one Good, one Justice, and so on. The man who discovers the nature of these Forms, and especially that of "the Good", ought to rule and ought to maintain his rule by a social system designed to preserve his class in power for ever.

"Platonism"—which may be defined as the adaptation of the theory of Forms to theology and ethics—has had a very great influence, especially in the field of religion, for most theologians have assumed that moral laws are absolute and objective, the same for all men, and that virtue is impossible apart from a knowledge of these objective moral laws. Christian philosophy up to the thirteenth century was entirely Platonic.

Plato has also been very influential in the field of pure philosophy, through his pioneering of the analysis of conceptions. This is the obverse of the definition of universals. When we define universal terms we try to abstract from a multitude of individuals that which they have in common. When we analyse abstract conceptions—terms such as "knowledge", "truth", "change"—we seek to define the range of different ideas subsumed in a single term. A great deal of philosophical speculation is reducible to analysis of conceptions, and it is with Plato that this branch of study originates.

5

PLATO'S PUPIL Aristotle is the third great figure in this flowering-time of Greek philosophy. He was born in Stagira in northern Greece in 384 B.C. and came to Athens to study at the Academy in 367. He stayed there until Plato's death in 347, when he left Athens and was for a time tutor of the young Alexander of Macedon. About 340 he returned to Athens and founded a second university, known as the Lyceum, which he conducted until 323 when, during a period of political trouble, he fled the city in case, as he put it, the Athenians should commit a second crime against philosophy—that is, execute Aristotle as they had Socrates. He died in Euboea in 322.

The surviving writings of Aristotle are the earliest "academic" philosophical treatises. They originate in notes made for his lectures over the whole of his teaching career and constitute a grand survey of the state of knowledge as it existed in Greece at that time, together with Aristotle's own speculations on every subject about which it was possible to hold an opinion. The influence of this body of writings has been immense and not wholly beneficial: in the field of physics in particular Aristotle's authority was constantly appealed to in medieval times to counter the "heresies" of empirical science, and his views on aesthetics, only partly understood, bedevilled the sensibilities of generations of artists and theorists from the time of the renaissance of dramatic art in the 16th century.

We shall consider here Aristotle's theories concerning the questions of form and matter, actuality and potential, the "causes" of existence and the Prime Mover—which are linked —and then his ethical theory.

Aristotle distinguishes the two aspects of all created things as form and matter. The matter of a thing is the material of which it is made, the form of a thing is its structure. For example, the matter of a book is paper, glue, ink, and so on, the form is the way in which this matter is put together to make a book. The matter of which forms are constructed is itself a form, since it is a structure made of some of the four "elements" fire, air, earth and water. Since these elements are capable of being changed one into another—water, for example, can become air—they are also forms of some primary matter which is without form. As there is matter without form

—although it is not present in the developed world—so there is form without matter. Form without matter is God.

These "forms" of Aristotle's have nothing in common with Plato's Forms: Aristotle does not believe in perfect prototypes existing in a "real" world. The form of a book is for him the observable structure of some existing book.

He also distinguishes the created world as potentiality and actuality. An acorn is the potentiality of an oak-tree, an oak-tree the actualisation of this potential. Matter is defined as that which has the potentiality of receiving form, form as that which actualises this potentiality. Any living thing is matter-and-form, potential-and-actualisation, body-and-soul. The soul—"psyche" —is the form of the body; a body which is capable of being alive is the potentiality of a living thing, the soul is the actualisation of this potentiality. The soul cannot exist apart from the body any more that the form of a table can exist apart from the actual table. There is therefore no "immortal soul".

Aristotle also proposes that any created thing should be described in terms of its four "causes": its material cause— what it is made of; its formal cause—its form or structure; its efficient cause—what made it; and its final cause—what its function or purpose is. This last "cause" distinguishes Aristotelean science and science influenced by Aristotle: it seeks to explain the world in part by understanding what its purpose can be—that is, it attempts a teleological explanation. This attitude was undoubtedly a retreat from the position adopted by the atomists, who offered a mechanical explanation without reference to purpose, and physical science did not advance very far until the teleological bias given it by Aristotle had been overcome through a return to the atomists.

Aristotle offers an argument in favour of the existence of what in his *Physics* he calls the "Prime Mover" and in his *Metaphysics* "God". The argument briefly is as follows. Change is empirically real, but we cannot imagine a first change, because every change presupposes something capable of being changed (matter or potentiality) and something capable of causing change (efficient cause or the power to actualise potentiality), and in addition some cause for this potentiality being actualised. This cause, whatever it is, must itself have been the consequence of a change, and so backwards in time. Change is therefore eternal, and to account for it we must posit a being which, itself unchanging, causes eternal change. This being is the Prime Mover, which is entirely form and actuality —that is, contains no matter and no unactualised potentialities. In the *Metaphysics*, Aristotle says that this supernal being must be pure activity, but a kind of activity which does not require time or change for its accomplishment. Pure intuitive thought is the activity of God and this activity constitutes what he is. What God thinks *about* is necessarily the highest object of thought, namely himself. God is therefore uninterrupted thinking about thinking.

Aristotle's ethical theory—expounded in his *Nicomachean Ethics*—rests upon his rejection of Plato's conception of the unique "Good", objectively real and the same for all men. "Good", says Aristotle, must be defined teleologically—that is, with reference to the function of the thing called good. A good bucket, for example, is a bucket which performs well the proper function of a bucket, which is to hold water. A good sword is one which performs well the proper functions of a sword, that is, one which is adequately sharp and hard and straight. And so on for every created thing. A good man is one who performs best the proper function of a man, and the proper function of a man—that which he can do best and which distinguishes him from the rest of creation—is to think, and the good life is the life consisting of actions which involve thought. Moral virtue, consequently, consists in the control of the passions by reason.

A man can learn to do this, and the better he has learned the better man he will be: at last he will act virtuously, not from constraint, but because he is happiest when virtuous. A man who is virtuous gladly is a better man—as well as a better-informed man—than one whose virtue requires effort. Thus Aristotle affirms the Socratic dictum that knowledge makes virtuous.

A famous passage of the *Nicomachean Ethics* describes the man of perfect virtue, whom Aristotle calls the "great-souled" or magnanimous man. Compared with the Christian saint, the magnanimous man is very proud and aloof, but from the point of view of Aristotle much in the Christian saint is abject. Ultimately, perhaps, which of them one prefers is a matter of taste, but the magnanimous man's virtues are largely defensible as "the golden mean" between two opposite vices: his pride, for example, is a mean between vanity (overestimation of oneself) and humility (underestimation of oneself) and may be defined as a realistic estimate of one's limitations on the one hand and the self-respect one owes to oneself on the other. The "doctrine of the mean" as a test of morality was one which Aristotle propounded with reservations. He was well aware that many moral actions cannot be defined as a mean between two vices: there is, for instance, no mean between telling the truth and telling lies. But he considered it a useful tool for determining the reasonable (and therefore virtuous) attitude on many moral questions.

Perhaps Aristotle's greatest achievement was his formulation of syllogistic logic or the logic of classes. This has been outlined in Part One of the present book and need not be repeated here. Aristotelean logic meant logic as such until the beginning of the present century, when it was replaced by the logic of propositions; but its limitations were recognised by Aristotle himself, who proposed it as a means of determining the logical truth of certain kinds of statement and not of all possible kinds of statement. His reputation as a dogmatist notwithstanding, he was a far more cautious theoriser than Plato.

Beyond any doubt, Aristotle possessed the greatest analytical mind the world has yet known. Socrates inspired imitation by living according to the lights of reason. Plato invited the world to philosophise and gave it its great philosophical model in a series of thrilling and dazzling works. But Aristotle, duller perhaps than these and more professorial, set philosophy on its feet and its feet on the ground. Western philosophy would have been possible (if very different) without Plato. Without Aristotle it is difficult to see how it could have come into existence at all.

6

DURING THE fourth century B.C. the world of the Greek city-states crumbled. Small-scale political units became a thing of the past, firstly with the victories of Alexander the Great, then with the rise of the Roman Empire. This decline in the political status of the city-state was accompanied by social and economic decay which led, among other things, to increased emigration from the Greek homeland and consequently the spread of Greek settlements and a rise in the Greek population in foreign cities throughout the Mediterranean world. The optimism of the age of Plato had gone. In its place there was a pervading sense of decline, of the best being in the past, and of defence-lessness before the new political and social powers. This period of Greek history is known as the Hellenistic Age (from the spread of indigenous Hellenic culture over a large part of the ancient world) and it was during this age that the philosophies called Cynicism, Stoicism and Epicureanism arose. What these philosophies have in common is that they are all directed at the individual and offer him an ethic by which he can endure the times in which he lives. They are all pessimistic concerning the possibility of a good life, and aim at supplying a recipe for as good a life as is still possible.

Stoicism and Epicureanism divided the ancient world between them philosophically from the end of the fourth century virtually until the dissolution of the Roman Empire. Both are very noble ethical doctrines capable of debasement by those understanding them only superficially. Stoicism debased becomes indifference to the sufferings of others and a fatalistic acceptance of social evil. Epicureanism debased becomes hedonism and a pursuit of the most immediate and crassest satisfactions. But in their pure state as they were understood by the best minds they provided philosophies adequate to the world in which they flourished. The popular conception of what is meant by a "philosophy"—a body of ethical and metaphysical teaching in the light of which one may live—derives ultimately from the age in which the Stoic and Epicurean philosophies, to which this definition applies precisely, dominated the thinking of a whole civilisation.

We shall here discuss the essential features of these two philosophies and of the sceptical movement which shadowed them. Firstly, however, we must look at the movement which preceded Stoicism and engendered it: the Cynicism of Diogenes.

Diogenes was one of the strangest figures of all antiquity. Expelled from his native Sinope, he lived stateless and penniless in Athens and Corinth, devoting his life to the public and practical expression of his philosophy, which was named Cynicism after Diogenes' nickname of "the Dog" (Greek *Kuon*). The story that he lived in a barrel is probably a joke, but he was certainly content with whatever shelter he could find, owned no property, despised wealth and deliberately flouted all convention and decency, apparently without the slightest fear of the consequences. Plato called him a Socrates gone mad, and the description does justice to the fantastic exaggeration in Diogenes of Socrates' hardihood and indifference to material comforts when these were not to be had without unreasonable effort. It is generally agreed that Diogenes' philosophy was derived from Antisthenes, who was a pupil of the sophist Gorgias and a friend of Socrates. Antisthenes taught the self-sufficiency of virtue and its incompatibility with wealth and luxury. The way to virtue was through knowledge and the acquisition of this knowledge the only important occupation of life. If an established convention conflicted with virtue it should be overthrown. Diogenes exaggerated this Socratic outlook to produce a philosophy of violent antagonism to everything usually considered worthwhile.

Self-sufficiency was the aim of the Cynic, and this implied not merely indifference to property and convention, but violent opposition. The self-sufficient life was a life in accordance with nature and this kind of life produced happiness. The Cynic philosophy of self-sufficiency is Socratic in so far as it offers to the individual an ethic through the practice of which he may attain virtue and, through virtue, happiness. Ethical considerations have overwhelmed all others: there is no Cynic metaphysic or theory of knowledge. Those considerations, which seemed so important to Plato and Aristotle, are ignored. The one thing needful is to discover a means by which men may be happy in a bad world. That this means is self-sufficiency follows from their incapacity to influence public events: only freedom from reliance on the outer world can ensure that one will remain virtuous and happy no matter what happens.

Diogenes is credited with some written works, but nothing survives and his teaching is clearly contained in his mode of living. It was capable of inspiring a genuine and noble asceticism, as in the famous case of Crates of Thebes, who, under the influence of Diogenes' practical teaching, parted with the whole of his considerable fortune and lived among the poor of Athens as doctor and adviser. But the baser sort of man could find in Cynicism an excuse for sneering denigration of qualities he did not himself possess and gave rise to the modern meaning of the word cynic.

It was through Crates that Zeno of Citium, in Cyprus, became acquainted with the Cynic philosophy and made it an integral part of his own philosophy.

Zeno came to Athens in 312 or 311 B.C. and studied at the Academy. He received from Crates' ethical example the impulse to original philosophising and founded his own school, where he taught a body of doctrine which came to be called "Stoicism" after the Painted Stoa (colonnade) in which he lectured. After his death in 262 he was succeeded as head of the Stoa by Cleanthes, who was in turn succeeded by Chrysippus in 232. Chrysippus, whose strength lay in logical argument and popularisation, gave new life and wider currency to Zeno's doctrines and made possible the development of Stoicism into something like a mass movement with a long-range effect. The system formulated by Chrysippus embodies contradictions which cannot be resolved, so that ultimately it must succumb to internal criticism; but its breadth was sufficiently wide to permit parts of it to be embraced in isolation, and it became an ennobling and humanising influence throughout the Graeco-Roman world. Such notably humane and enlightened thinkers as the freed slave Epictetus and the emperor Marcus Aurelius were Stoics. Parts of the Stoic doctrine, especially the logic and the physics, are of antiquarian interest only, but the ethical and metaphysical doctrines are concerned with philosophical problems still entirely relevant, and it is these we shall consider.

Stoic ethics derived from Cynicism and embodied the view that virtue is the one thing which will enable a man to be happy whatever his external circumstances may be, and that virtue consists in living in harmony with nature. Before one can do this, one must know what living in harmony with nature implies, and thus Stoicism reaffirms the dictum of Socrates that knowledge makes virtuous.

The Stoic conception of nature is not easy to grasp, because it is based on an outmoded physics, but its metaphysical implications can be stated quite simply : the material world is penetrated in all its parts by the *logos* or eternal rational principle, which is divine and which exercises absolute control over all events and directs the universe; human reason is an aspect of the divine *logos* and man is therefore capable of dis-covering the rational principles which determine and guide the world and of living in accordance with them; to live in accordance with the *logos* is to live in harmony with nature and this constitutes virtue and brings happiness. The develop-ment of the moral intelligence is the learning of wisdom and thus philosophy is the way not only to knowledge, but also to virtue. The wise man (if he is a pupil of the Stoa) will know the rational laws of nature and how to act in accordance with them in any given instance.

Whatever clouds the moral intelligence or hinders it in its search for the laws of reason is to be avoided, since it can lead only to error, consequently to unvirtue, consequently to un-happiness. The passions, conceived as external forces operating upon the mind, must be subordinated to reason and not permitted to influence rational judgment. If this is not done, reason will err and this will lead to decisions not in accordance with virtue. The troubles and trials of life must be borne with equanimity, since the divine *logos* has ordered that things shall be as they are and to resist is irrational and (consequently) unvirtuous.

Stoic metaphysics, embodying as it does the notion that divine reason permeates and directs all things, leads to a rigid determinism: what will be, will be. Since the *logos* is conceived of as divine, it must direct all things for the best: what seems like evil cannot, ultimately, be real evil but must be conducive to good. These metaphysical postulates are inconsistent with the ethical doctrines, which involve freewill and the possibility of moral error, which is unvirtue and must therefore be in some way evil. Chrysippus' attempts to resolve these contradictions are unsuccessful and fail to answer the basic objection that, if all events are predetermined, it is vain to urge men to become virtuous (i.e. Stoics) since what they will be, they will be. In the Stoic philosophy we encounter for the first time one of the fundamental problems of morals: we may wish that men were better (as we conceive better) and urge them to change their characters, and we cannot logically do this unless we suppose them to possess at least some degree of freewill; but to demonstrate the existence of freewill has so far proved very difficult. The evidence in favour of determinism is very strong; yet when the Stoics accepted it and decreed an absolute determinism, they found it made their ethical teaching nonsensical and illogical. If other moral teachers have avoided this impasse, it has hitherto been by what must in all strictness be called an act of faith: they have *believed* in freewill because they have believed in moral responsibility, which cannot exist without it. But this belief is not founded on "fact": such "facts" as there are speak in favour of determinism. The contradictions which here arise—and which a man of strong moral *and* intellectual conscience will find very painful—is exposed in the most glaring manner in the failure of the Stoics to reconcile a belief in strict determinism with a belief in the perfectability of man.

The philosophy called Epicureanism, after its founder Epicurus, was more modest in its aims than Stoicism and, perhaps for that reason, more obviously attractive and sound. Epicurus, who was born in Athens in 342 B.C., founded his school there in about 306. He taught in a garden attached to his house and his school was therefore sometimes referred to as "the Garden" (as Zeno's school was referred to as "the Stoa", Plato's as "the Academy", and Aristotle's as "the Lyceum"). He is credited with having written 300 books and, whether or not this was an exaggeration, he was certainly a voluminous writer, although less than 100 pages of his works survive. Epicurus in his garden, teaching his pupils and writing his 300 books, became a symbol of philosophic imperturbability and withdrawal, and the feature of Epicureanism which divides it most markedly from Stoicism is its private and personal character. Stoicism became a philosophy for practical men, particularly statesmen and those with great responsibilities, Epicureanism a philosophy of retreat and self-containedness.

Epicurus was not an original thinker: he derived both his physics and his ethics from Democritus. But he gave Democritus' theories popular appeal and made of them a philosophy of life acceptable to many generations of thinkers. Epicurean physics has already been discussed—it is atomism with slight modifications—and we shall confine ourselves here to the ethics.

The basis of Epicurus' morals is that pleasure alone is good. There are two kinds of pleasure: physical and mental. Physical pleasure consists in the abolition of pain, mental pleasure in the abolition of fear and anxiety. Wisdom consists in knowing how to abolish pain, fear and anxiety, and knowledge is therefore necessary for the achievement of virtue. Perfect health and clear rationality are the highest good and at the same time the source of the highest happiness. As a practical ethic, these doctrines imply moderation in physical pleasures, since these bring pain with them; the overcoming of superstition and the fear of death; and clear thinking about all things. Epicurus' day-to-day teaching was chiefly concerned with the exercise of clear thinking in the choice of pleasures.

Epicureanism as a moral doctrine may be called a form of rational hedonism: pleasure is the only good, but not all pleasures are good, because some pleasures are attended or followed by pain, and one must therefore know how to distinguish good pleasures from bad ones. The somewhat paradoxical consequence is that the "philosophy of pleasure" was in practice a rather austere discipline which if it taught the avoidance of hardship, also taught abstemiousness and firm self-control. But the paradox is only an apparent one, if the nature of real pleasure is considered seriously in a world in which pain, discomfort and fear are far more common than unalloyed pleasure. In such a world, property, for example, came to be an ambiguous advantage, since one will always be afraid of losing it: in this instance, the abolition of pain (in the form of hunger, destitution, sickness and so on) which the possession of property accomplishes undoubtedly at least in part, is achieved only at the cost of increased mental displeasure (in the form of fear). It is undoubtedly a good thing to own *some* property, but it should be in the form symbolised by Epicurus' garden: just sufficient and unostentatious (for ostentation is an invitation to envy and there are good grounds for fearing the envious man). But in no case should one's pleasure of body or mind be *dependent* upon property or upon anything over which one has no certain control; and this consideration rules out excess of any kind. Epicureanism is thus seen to be at one with Cynicism and Stoicism in offering to man a philosophy of self-sufficiency in a bad world.

7

THROUGHOUT THE Hellenistic Age, the positive philosophies we have been considering had to contend with the very widespread and ably argued Sceptical movement which originated with Pyrrho of Elis about 300 B.C. Scepticism, as a philosophical term, means the view that there is a limit to the possibility of knowledge. This view has been held, with differences of emphasis, from the time of Pyrrho to the present day, and most of its variants can be seen in the Hellenic Sceptics. Because of the importance of the Sceptical attitude for the whole history of philosophy, we would be well-advised to consider these opinions and arguments in some detail.

The Scepticism of Pyrrho was offered as a rebuttal of the dogmatism of Stoicism and Epicureanism and as an alternative philosophy of happiness. Pyrrho considered the object of philosophy to be the attainment of detachment and tranquillity, and in this he was in accord with the tendency of his age. But the existence of conflicting dogmatisms—principally Stoicism and Epicureanism—suggested to him that the search for truth was vain. There were, he said, no objective criteria for distinguishing between true and false sense perceptions or for deciding which of several conflicting judgments was the right one. Certain knowledge was impossible, and since this was so, the search for it conflicted with the end philosophy was designed to serve, namely the attainment of tranquillity. Therefore the search for knowledge must be given up, and one must learn to live in a state of suspended judgment. Thus, in Pyrrho, an epistemological theory (one cannot know the truth) leads to a moral theory (one ought not to seek the truth). But the moral theory is weak, since it fails to offer any guide to positive action, and it was as an attack on dogmatic theories of knowledge that the Sceptical movement made its greatest impact in the generation after Pyrrho, when it captured Plato's Academy and produced a succession of very able and very modern-sounding philosophers whose chief concern was to attack philosophic dogmatism of any kind, but especially Stoic dogmatism.

The Sceptics of the Academy developed an historically important technique for advancing Sceptical opinions: that of arguing for and against any question with equal plausibility. This technique was adopted by Kant when he wished to demonstrate the impossibility of constructive metaphysics.

The greatest of the Academic Sceptics was Carneades of

Cyrene, who was born seven years before the death of Chrysippus, whose system he was considered by many to have utterly destroyed. If one accepts the arguments of Carneades, nothing in the Stoic philosophy remains credible. He argued that there is no criterion in sensation itself to enable one to distinguish false sense perceptions from true ones; that reason derives ultimately from sense perceptions and therefore the judgments arrived at by reason are vitiated by the unreliability of these perceptions; and that moral responsibility involves free will.

From the first century B.C. onwards Scepticism flourished chiefly outside the Academy, and Sceptical thinkers such as Aenesidemus and Agrippa attained to a very high degree of skill in the dialectical demolition of dogmatic theory. A systematic account of Scepticism as a philosophical outlook was produced which is in some ways the most valuable exercise in pure philosophy to emerge from the Hellenistic Age. We cannot go into all its details here, but a few examples will show the kind of analysis the later Sceptics produced.

Disagreements between philosophers cannot be resolved, they maintained, because no criteria exist for resolving them, only the opinions of other philosophers. Sense perception is relative, not pure, and depends upon the nature of the perceiver, of the object perceived, and of the attendant circumstances: an object cannot be perceived at all as it really is. The concept of causality is not founded upon sense perception but is a series of assumptions which cannot be confirmed by observation. The later Sceptics even attacked the Sceptics of the Academy for being too dogmatic: to deny the possibility of knowledge was held to be a piece of dogmatism for which no warrant could be discovered in reason: one had to be sceptical even about Scepticism.

The entire Sceptical outlook was summarised by Sextus Empiricus late in the second century A.D. During the third century the movement expired. By this date, the morale of the Empire had declined so far that only a philosophy of uplift and escape stood any chance of widespread acceptance, and this was offered by the so-called Platonic revival of Plotinus ("so-called" because the Plato of Plotinus is not the real Plato): the total disenchantment of Scepticism was the last thing that was wanted. But although this movement in classical philosophy passed away, scepticism as such remains a fundamental trait in all analytical philosophy and is as lively today as ever. It is one of the most valuable gifts we have received from the Greeks.

8

IT HAS often been remarked that classical antiquity—the world of Greece and Rome in their heyday—seems nearer to us than the chronologically later period of the collapse of the Empire and the age of intellectual darkness which followed it. Julius Caesar seems more modern and comprehensible than Charlemagne. This sensation is also experienced in philosophy. Although much in Plato, Aristotle and their successors of the Hellenistic Age seems strange and even fantastic to us, we are conscious of inhabiting the same intellectual world as these thinkers. The doctrines of the Academy, the Lyceum, the Stoa and the Garden are designed to meet difficulties we ourselves experience, and the Sceptical movement of late antiquity in particular is concerned with very "modern" philosophical problems. But the philosophy of the late Empire and of Christian Europe to the 13th century is not in the least "modern", and to feel at home in it requires a great effort of imagination.

This age was dominated philosophically by neo-Platonism and theologically by Christianity and the overriding characteristic of the Christian age from our point of view is the attempt to reconcile religious dogma with classical philosophy, represented mainly by neo-Platonism. There was no sudden break, and it cannot even be said that Christian apologists adapted Greek philosophical ideas to suit their requirements, for this adaptation had already been accomplished by the last great philosopher of antiquity, Plotinus. The continuity of the tradition is symbolised by the fact that Plotinus and the first

great Christian philosopher, Origen, were pupils of the same
master, Ammonius Saccas. The novel element in the new
situation appears when Origen's views are declared "heretical"
by the Christian establishment, a fate which could not have
befallen Plotinus, since he was not a Christian. With Plotinus,
the age of untrammelled speculation comes to an end; with
Origen, the age of orthodoxy and heresy begins. It is this
distinction, and not any break in the philosophical tradition,
which divides classical from Catholic philosophy.

The ultimate philosophical system of antiquity, now known
as neo-Platonism, is in intention a synthesis of all previous
systems except Epicureanism, which is rejected. In reality,
neo-Platonism ignores a very great deal of what seems to us of
value in the Greeks, and especially in Plato, whose philosophy
the neo-Platonists supposed they were essentially reviving.
Plato's theory of Forms and his tendency to mysticism are
almost all the neo-Platonists used. His dialectics, his discussion
of the nature of virtue, and his analysis of conceptions are
omitted. The sceptical element in Greek philosophy, which
dates back to Xenophanes and sometimes seems to be the most
valuable, as it is certainly the most "modern" intellectual
achievement of the Greeks, has no place in neo-Platonism
either, and this fact helps us to see what this final philosophy
of the ancient world essentially was: a union of Plato's other-
worldliness and the urge to self-sufficiency in a bad world which
characterised the post-Aristotelean movements, both driven to
an extreme. The classic exposition of neo-Platonism is the series
of treatises called the *Enneads*, written by Plotinus and edited
by his disciple, Porphyry. To read the *Enneads* and then to read
Gibbon's account of the history of the years during which they
were written is to understand why Plotinus became one of the
most influential of all philosophers. The third century A.D.
was an age of utter ruin for the Empire. The whole world—for
to the ancients the Empire and the world were the same thing—
seemed to be in a state of collapse, and contemplation of it
could only bring a sense of hopelessness and disgust. The
antidote to this was a philosophy which asserted that the "real"

world, of which the world of sense was only a distorted reflection, was a realm of beauty and order, and that man might, through moral and intellectual effort, get in touch with this real world. This message is the heart of Plotinus' metaphysical philosophy and the source of its great influence. The Christian conception of the nature of reality owes a tremendous amount to neo-Platonism, and especially the concept that the "real" world—the beyond, the Kingdom of Heaven—is the *opposite* of the mundane world: *here* is darkness and sorrow, *there* is light and joy. This outlook, which formed the ground of the theological consciousness of the first Christian millennium, was derived immediately from Plotinus and was perhaps the psychological saving of a civilisation which came very near to total disintegration, just as it was responsible for the almost total neglect of social questions during the same period. In the fulness of his very beautiful system, Plotinus does not turn away from the world, he seeks to illumine and justify it. But the superiority of the other world is so firmly insisted upon and its beauty and goodness so powerfully described, that to the minds of his followers he seemed to offer an object of contemplation which lifted them above the darkness and decay of their mundane existence. Neo-Platonism, as a popular force, had all the ingredients of a religion except a God: when Christianity supplied one, the combination virtually obliterated all other philosophies and religions and ruled as sole truth for Western man for nearly a thousand years.

It is neither possible nor necessary to go far into Plotinus' system here. It is not very obscure but it is complicated and unless explained in detail is likely to seem fantastic. It deals with the fundamental metaphysical question of the nature of being. Beyond, above and outside everything is the "One" from which being emanates as light emanates from the sun. The One can be imagined as God, provided one does not picture it as a person or ascribe to it any attributes. Plotinus says we should say of it only that "It is"—but since it transcends being, perhaps we should not say even that. Subordinate to the One is Spirit (*Nous*), which is the One's knowledge of itself. Below

Spirit is Soul, which is the creator of all things, living and inanimate. The world it creates is a copy of the divine world, the evil in the world being the faults inherent in a copy. Through instruction and virtuous living, man, as a creation of the Soul, may get in touch with the *Nous*, the divine emanation. Plotinus declared he had often done so in states of ecstacy, yet there is very little superstition in him—astoundingly little for a man of his era. He is a uniquely-impressive combination of metaphysician and mystic.

It was dangerously easy to envisage Plotinus' trinity of One, Spirit and Soul as the Holy Trinity of God the Father, Son and Holy Ghost—"dangerously" because the members of Plotinus' trinity are not equals and when Origen sought to interpret the Christian dogma of the Trinity in neo-Platonic terms, his views were declared heretical for this reason.

Catholic Philosophy

RELIGIOUS BELIEF and free speculation go ill together and during the age of absolute Christian domination—very roughly from A.D. 600 to 1500—secular philosophy ceased to exist. The chief intellectual discipline was theology, and it is a matter of some difficulty to separate theological from philosophical inquiry during this long period. What distinguishes the Christian philosopher from his counterpart in Greece and Rome is that he believes in an historical divine revelation of truth, which is accepted by faith: he *knows* the truth *before* he begins to philosophise. This might seem to be the arch-sin against philosophy and, indeed, to make philosophy impossible; but this is not literally so: what it means is that philosophy approximates to theology and becomes a means rather than an end in itself. One tries to justify faith by reason; and part of one's faith is that reason *will* justify it. But the situation is complicated by the concept of orthodoxy: certain views are declared correct and thenceforward outside the sphere of speculation; certain other views are declared incorrect and the faithful are forbidden to hold them. The holding of views declared incorrect is called heresy, and the punishment for heresy is exclusion from the Christian community, in this world and the next. Thus, intellectual error comes to be equated with moral turpitude and to be mistaken is to be sinful. The effect this authoritarianism would have upon free speculation is self-evident and it is not surprising that free speculation almost ceased in Western Europe until the revival of secular philosophy in the 16th and 17th centuries.

Catholic philosophy falls into two big periods, early and late.

The early period is from the beginning of the second century A.D. until about 600; the late period from about 1000 to the Renaissance. Between 600 and 1000 lie the correctly-named Dark Ages, during which intellectual activity was virtually at a stop in Europe. During the early period, Christian and non-Christian philosophy existed side-by-side and both were to a great extent dominated by the contemporary view of Plato, that is, by neo-Platonism. During the late period, non-Christian philosophy was not permitted to exist, and Christian philosophers were to a great extent dominated by the contemporary view of Aristotle. The climax of the whole movement came in the thirteenth century, during which the most complete synthesis possible of classical philosophy and Christian theology was achieved by Thomas Aquinas.

2

THE FIRST Christian who was also a philosopher of note was Origen (born A.D. 185, died 254). We have already seen that his philosophical training was identical with that of the last great philosopher of Greece, Plotinus; and his outlook will seem very strange to us unless we grasp that it was formed from an attempted fusion of classical philosophy as he understood it (i.e. neo-Platonism) and Christian dogma in the incomplete condition in which it then existed. Origen shows us the most attractive side of primitive Christianity. He believes in the truth of the gospel, and that philosophy will vindicate his belief. He thinks that opponents of Christianity should be argued with, not sent to Hell. Origen's metaphysics combines certain fantastic beliefs—such as that the stars have souls and in the efficacy of magic—with what is fundamentally Plotinus' system. In a famous book, *Against Celsus*, he makes an effort to answer the philosophical objections to Christianity raised by a "pagan" philosopher, Celsus, maintaining that the gospels would appear true to anyone who read them with a knowledge of Greek philosophy, but that, in addition, they were divinely inspired and carried their own conviction. This two-fold source of knowledge—philosophical thought and divine revelation—is the fundamental characteristic of all Catholic knowledge. In Origen it first becomes explicit.

The foregoing ought not to suggest that Origen was in any way lukewarm in his faith. The contrary is true. He was fanatically convinced of the divinity of Jesus and of the obligation Jesus' followers had to follow his commandments. Interpreting correctly but over-literally the significance of Jesus' dictum "If thy eye offend thee, pluck it out", he emasculated himself, an act which implies the firmest belief in that Heaven promised to those who successfully resisted the world and the flesh.

Christian theology in Origen's day was not fully developed and he felt under no constraint to conform to it: this led him to what was later condemned as heresy. One of his heresies was that God the Father is superior to God the Son, who is superior to God the Holy Ghost—a Christian formulation of Plotinus' trinity. He also taught, following Plato, that souls exist before birth as well as after death, a view later declared heretical.

In the following century, orthodoxy hardened, and Augustine, who was born exactly 100 years after Origen's death (354) and died in 430, was continually obsessed with the need to conform to the "truth". Augustine was perhaps the most influential of all Christian teachers, but most of his teaching lies outside philosophy and belongs to theology and Church doctrine. Philosophically he was, like most of his contemporaries, under the influence of Plato, and it was in Platonic terminology that he formulated his theories of "divine ideas" and "divine illumination". There exist eternal facts, he said, such as the facts of mathematics, which are independent of any human mind and would be true whether or not there existed any human mind to know them. But if they do not originate in a human mind, where do they originate? In the eternal mind, the mind of God: they are divine "ideas", and this is evidence for the existence of God. There also exist eternal standards, such as those of absolute beauty, justice, and so on, to which human attainments are understood to approximate more or less closely. These standards, which have no existence in the mundane world, are Forms in the Platonic sense. They are apprehended, not through the senses, but by "divine illumination" of the intellect. Augustine was not concerned with discovering proofs of God's existence, failing which he might suspend belief in God. Belief came first and was not troubled by doubt; philosophy was a kind of voyage of discovery, an approach to God by reason.

Augustine was the greatest philosopher of the fifth century and the only one remembered at all widely today, although he is remembered chiefly as a theologian and as the author of the *Confessions*, an account of his own early life coloured by his later conversion to Christianity. His principal theological work is the famous *City of God*, which gave permanent literary expression to the fundamental dualism of the Christian faith, whose social form is the dualism of Church and state, and whose transcendental form is the dualism of this world and the next. His theology had a very great and long-range effect: it was the main theoretical inspiration of the Reformation. To a non-Christian it seems ferociously inhuman, indeed in parts hardly sane. Its picture of the world as a brief stopping-place between non-existence and an eternity of well-merited torment, with the gratuitous gift of eternal joy for a tiny minority of the elect, is one of the most appalling ever to enter the mind of man. Yet there is no escaping the fact that Augustine's theology was for many centuries Christian theology as such, nor that when the Catholic Church began to discard it, the Reformation gave it new life in Protestantism. Luther venerated Augustine as the one true Doctor of the Church, and Calvin was an extreme Augustinian.

The world of Augustine was still recognisably the old Roman world, however decayed and bedraggled; but during the fifth century that old world vanished. In the year 800 Charlemagne was crowned Holy Roman Emperor and a new order began slowly to emerge. By 1000 the feudal system was established. Whatever its defects, it did restore form and solidity to a shapeless society and intellectual life could begin anew. But for the relatively huge period of nearly 500 years philosophy was almost extinct in Western Europe, and might very well have expired altogether, along with the art of writing and the science of numbers, if the monastic system had not kept them tenuously alive. The monasteries were oases of civilised life in a desert of barbarism and it is to them, despite all their short-comings in theory and practice, that we owe the survival of classical learning.

Only one philosopher of the sixth century is remembered today: Boethius (born about 480, died 524), the author of *On the Consolation of Philosophy*, which was for a thousand years the supreme model of philosophic reflection and discourse. King Alfred translated it into English in the ninth century, and Chaucer translated it again in the fourteenth. Written in prison while Boethius was awaiting execution on a treason charge, it is one of the world's great books and one of the very few produced in Western Europe which invite comparison with the Platonic and Aristotelean classics. Boethius intended to translate into Latin and comment upon all the works of Aristotle, but completed only the *Logic*. In the field of epistemology he was important for his specific formulation of a problem which engaged much of the attention of medieval philosophers: the problem of universals. He posed the question "whether *genera* and *species* actually subsist or are found in the mind and intellect alone," and this was the form in which the problem of universals presented itself to the medieval mind.

Five years after Boethius' death the philosophical schools of Athens were closed by the Christian emperor Justinian, and night fell on the intellect of Europe. The teaching of philosophy ceased, empirical science vanished almost from mind, and mere literacy became a rare accomplishment. The classical world was stigmatised as "pagan" and sent to damnation. The Greek language was almost lost. Superstitions which would have made the contemporaries of Julius Caesar stare in disbelief were universally credited and became historical forces. From the highest to the lowest, Western man was existing in mental darkness. The idea of purposeful state-building—almost an obsession of the Greeks and Romans—was blotted out by the theological preoccupation of those who might, under more propitious circumstances, have led the way to a cleaner and saner life on earth: power was contested between vigorous but illiterate barbarians and literate but otherworld-orientated clerics, and between them they made of Europe the most desolate cultural wasteland in recorded history.

The Dark Ages produced one philosopher: Johannes Erigena or John the Scot. (Erigena means "of Ireland" and in the Middle Ages the name "Scot" was used to denote an inhabitant of Ireland). He was born about 810 and died about 877 and is very remarkable as a man of the ninth century. Erigena was an Irish monk; the monasteries of Ireland preserved more of ancient learning than those on the Continent and were almost the only places in Chistendom in which Greek was known. He translated philosophical texts from Greek—a unique achievement in his century—and produced a metaphysical system which is an outstanding example of an attempt to fuse Christian theology and neo-Platonism. He finds four stages in "Nature"—by which he means the whole of reality. The first is "Nature which creates and is not created", which constitutes God; the second "Nature which is created and creates", which constitutes the eternal divine Forms or Ideas; the third "Nature which is created and does not create", which constitutes finite creatures. A fourth and final stage subsumes the first three as "Nature which neither creates nor is created", which is the oneness of all things with God in the last accounting. The similarity to the neo-Platonic system is obvious.

Erigena's system is set out in his book *On the Division of Nature*. It had no influence on his own generation, but became very famous during the twelfth century and in the thirteenth was declared heretical. He was born in an age which had no idea how to appreciate his gifts and he stands as perhaps the most isolated figure in the history of philosophy.

3

THE REVIVAL of learning from the late tenth century onwards took place entirely within church and monastic discipline, and later within that of the religious orders. None of it was secular in the modern sense : teachers and students were alike members of some religious body. The universities of the Middle Ages comprised a body of teachers and students active within a single city; when such a "university" was granted a charter it was constituted a corporation, with corporate status and privileges. The older universities were not "founded", but developed gradually, so it is impossible to assign them a starting date : the most important in the thirteenth century was the university of Paris, which developed during the second half of the twelfth century and received its charter in the year 1200; Oxford and Cambridge developed slightly later, but Bologna received its charter as early as 1158, and the school of Chartres—a single body and not a university—was founded in 990. The purposeful foundation of universities began in the thirteenth century : Heidelberg was founded in 1386, Cologne in 1389, Erfurt in 1392, Cracow in 1397, Leipzig in 1409, Louvain in 1425. In addition, many large abbeys were also centres of learning.

The union of philosophy and theology as taught and studied by churchmen at all these establishments during the Middle Ages is known as "scholasticism"—i.e. learning in a school—and its practitioners are commonly called "schoolmen". The philosophy of the schoolmen, whatever its colour, was invariably founded on logic as then understood, that is, on the logic of Aristotle. Boethius had translated Aristotle's *Logic* back in the sixth century; the recovery of the remainder of Aristotle and of much of the other Greek philosophers (but not Plato) was made possible by its preservation in Islam. During the centuries of darkness in Christendom, the Mohammedan world had enjoyed an age of high culture. Much of Greek philosophy was translated into Syriac, and from Syriac into Arabic, in which language it exercised great influence. During the twelfth century, the Arabic versions were translated into Latin, and so became current in Europe. At the same time, a knowledge of Greek began to be more general, and some philosophical works were translated into Latin directly from the Greek originals. It was in this way that, by the thirteenth century, Aristotle was available in Latin almost complete (although some works not by him were attributed to him) and became the principal influence in Western philosophy: to Thomas Aquinas, the greatest of the schoolmen, Aristotle is simply "the Philosopher".

But the old tradition of neo-Platonism and Augustine's metaphysics contrived to maintain itself side-by-side with the Aristotelean teaching and one way of making vivid the philosophical movements within scholasticism is to distinguish them according to whether Aristotle or Augustine is the predominating influence. Plato was known only in the one-sided version presented by neo-Platonism. It was not until the Renaissance that his dialogues were translated in any number: the most important were unknown to the Middle Ages. Only the *Timaeus* was available before the twelfth century, and the thirteenth and fourteenth added only two or three more of the shorter dialogues. This meant not only that the schoolmen had no knowledge of much of what we value most in Plato, but perhaps more importantly, that they had no real knowledge of Socrates, the man who stands for us in the same relation to reason as Christ does to faith.

The transmission of Greek philosophy to the west—and principally the philosophy of Aristotle—was also facilitated through the translation into Latin of the works of the great Arab philosophers Avicenna (Ibn Sina, 980-1037) and Averroes (Ibn Rusd, 1126-1198), and Jewish philosophers Avicebron (Salomon Ibn Gabiroc, about 1021-1069) and Moses Maimomides (1135-1204). The thinking of all these philosophers was founded upon Aristotle, with greater or less influence from neo-Platonism and some attempt (not very successful) to accommodate these sources to Mohammedan or Jewish orthodoxy.

As we have already said, the schoolmen were first and fore-most believing Christians and practising theologians, and one might ask what, in that event, they wanted from philosophy. The answer is provided by Anselm (1037-1109), who said he philosophised in order to understand his beliefs. First came belief, then the attempt to understand by reason the facts believed. It is therefore quite comprehensible that one of the major preoccupations of scholastic philosophy was the devising of proofs for the existence of God. In a book called the *Mono-logium*, Anselm presents arguments for God's existence founded on the neo-Platonic conception of degrees of perfec-tion. Anselm argues that no created being is perfect in any respect, e.g. no one is perfectly good, but that all are perfect to a certain degree. They must derive this degree of perfection from a being which is that perfection in an absolute sense, and that being is God. His most influential argument in this field is the so-called ontological argument (i.e. the argument based on the nature of being), presented in the *Proslogium*. All beings are perfect to a greater or less degree, says Anselm, so it is logical to suppose that there exists a most perfect being, the being "than which no greater can be thought". If this being is defined as "God", then God must exist, since if God were only an idea, existing only in the mind, it would be possible to imagine a more perfect being, that is, one existing in reality, and this would be a contradiction. We are compelled by logic, there-fore, to think that an absolutely perfect being actually exists, therefore that God exists. This argument is a first-rate example of the tendency of the schoolmen to equate logic and reality, to think that what is logically true *must* be true in the real world.

The ontological proof of God's existence was rejected by Thomas Aquinas, by Kant and by most post-Kantian philosophers. The most forceful objection is that existence is not a predicate and it therefore makes no sense to say that a being of which existence is predicated is "more perfect" than an imaginary being. It should be added that there is general agreement to reject as inadequate *all* the arguments for God's existence which have been put forward, including the five famous arguments of Thomas to be described shortly.

Another major interest of the schoolmen, especially those of Anselm's generation and the next, was the problem of universals, which had been given its characteristic form by Boethius. The question at issue was whether universal concepts and terms are or are not descriptions of actually-existing entities. Those who held that they are were called "realists". They argued that a positive reality exists to correspond to every name, therefore that the names of universal concepts must describe something real. This view in an extreme was that a universal essence or substance exists in reality to correspond to every universal concept in the mind, and this leads to the idea that there exists in reality one substance or being, and one only, of which all individual substances or beings are modifications. The system of Erigena tends towards this view, and was the chief reason it was declared heretical.

The opposing viewpoint, which was ultimately victorious, was that only individuals exist and that universal terms are a "gathering together" or abstraction; that there are, for instance, individual men, and the universal term "man" is an abstraction taken from observed similarities in individuals. Those holding this opinion were called "nominalists". They argued that universal terms do not exist in reality but are only mental concepts.

The controversy between realists and nominalists reached its climax in the dispute between William of Champeaux (died 1120) and Peter Abelard (1079-1142). William was an extreme realist, Abelard in reality a moderate realist but so far removed from William as to appear to contemporaries a champion of nominalism. The outcome of the dispute was the victory of Abelard, with William renouncing his position in favour of moderate realism and the nominalists feeling that their viewpoint had won the day. Abelard was one of the most important philosophers of the Middle Ages, especially for his influence on the method by which philosophy was taught by the later schoolmen. In his book *Yes and No* he collected together apparently contradictory opinions from the writings of the Church Fathers with the object of discussing them and seeing if the contradictions could be resolved: this method of pursuing philosophy by quoting conflicting opinions and then giving one's own view of the matters discussed was practised very widely in the schools of the thirteenth and fourteeth centuries, and forms the basis of much of Thomas's work. (Kant's critical metaphysics proceeds by a similar method.)

Abelard also gave new impetus to ethical philosophy, which had been neglected by thinkers to whom "good and evil" seemed to be fixed and final. In *Know Thyself*—a title which suggests Abelard's affinity with a side of Greek philosophy strange to most medieval philosophers—he argues that intention is the moral factor in moral actions: an act is good if the intention is good, since the intention is all that can be under the control of the doer of the action. Morality, according to Abelard, *consists* of good intentions: the "good" act is outside morality and adds nothing moral to the intention. Thus, literally any act may be good if the doer had good intentions, and any action bad if the doer had bad intentions. This view is the exact opposite of the later ethical philosophy known as "utilitarianism", according to which an act is good if it is conducive to the greatest good of the greatest number, the intention of the doer being irrelevant. Both views are easy to criticise. In neither case can we really know whether to approve or disapprove of an act, in the former because we cannot know the intention of the doer (sometimes he does not really know it himself), and in the latter because we cannot be certain what the ultimate effect of any act will be and therefore we cannot know if it will be conducive to the greatest good of the greatest number. We are likely to forgive the perpetrator of a harmful act if we feel certain his intentions were good, and we are not likely to criticise very severely a man who does a good act because we suspect his intentions were not of the purest. But in both cases it seems that something more is required for us to declare the entire event—intention and action—unequivocally good.

Although Anselm and Abelard were both churchmen and

devout believers, their interest in philosophy was perfectly sincere and as disinterested as it could be given their dogmatic presuppositions. But there were many theologians who thought philosophy misleading or a waste of time, and the impulse to philosophical speculation might not have withstood the attacks upon it had the religious orders not devoted themselves to it. During the thirteenth and fourteenth centuries almost all the well-known philosophers were either Franciscans or Dominicans who learned and taught at the great abbeys or at the new universities.

The Franciscans were as a whole orientated towards Augustine, the Dominicans towards Aristotle. Since Aristotle's philosophy was a relative novelty, the Dominicans counted as "advanced" thinkers, the Franciscans as "conservative". The great figure of the Franciscan order in the mid-thirteenth century was Bonaventure (1221-1274), whose philosophy combines respect for Aristotle's logic and theory of knowledge with rejection of his metaphysics. Metaphysically, Bonaventure was a follower of Augustine and, like him, believed that final metaphysical truths were obtainable only through revelation: that is, he assimilated metaphysics to theology.

An English Franciscan who stands apart in his age as an advocate of empirical observation and scientific method was Roger Bacon (born about 1212, died after 1292). He was especially interested in optics and worked out in theory how a telescope might be made. To the uneducated he appeared a dangerous man, probably in league with the Devil. The union of practical science and theoretical speculation in one head was a rarity in the medieval world, in which empiricism—philosophical and practical—was almost non-existent. Bacon called attention to the necessity of keeping one's ideas in check by referring them to the facts of the observable world.

The chief philosopher of the Dominicans and the undisputed master of Catholic theology is Thomas Aquinas (born about 1225, died 1274), whose achievement was to make a synthesis of Aristotle's philosophy and Christian theology which has proved durable and is still the theoretical basis of Catholic teaching. He distorted Aristotle in doing so, but this was inevitable since he could not distort Christian teaching and the two are not perfectly compatible. It follows that Thomas was not an original philosopher. His outlook agrees with that of Aristotle and his philosophical influence consisted in giving Aristotle's views almost canonical authority. His most important works are the *Summa contra Gentiles* and the later *Summa Theologica*. The former is of greater interest philosophically, as it is directed at those not already Christians, but the latter is his masterpiece and constitutes the summit of the scholasticist achievement.

Thomas is the king of theologians, but as a philosopher he is not of the front rank. He is in a sense insincere in the arguments he puts foward to sustain his conclusions, since these conclusions have already been arrived at by faith and will not be abandoned if the arguments can be demonstrated unsound (as they can be). Those which are founded on Aristotle are weakened by a linguistic confusion, the surmounting of which is one of the few positive advances in philosophy since his day; this is particularly true of his lengthy discussion of Aristotle's problems of matter and form, potentiality and actuality, which in Thomas becomes the problem of essence and existence.

In simple terms, the essence of a thing is its essential nature, that which it essentially is; its existence is the actualisation of this essence. In his analysis of the essence-existence problem, Thomas tries to show that there is nothing in the essence of any finite being which obliges it to exist; that is, we can imagine any finite being as not existing. This means that all finite beings must be brought into existence, and are therefore dependent and contingent. And *this* means that there must exist a being not dependent or contingent which is the first cause of all finite being and whose essense involves existence. No finite being necessarily exists, but God necessarily exists, and in him essence and existence are one.

In the *Summa Theologica*, Thomas offers five proofs of the existence of God. The first four are founded upon the supposition, derived from Aristotle, that a series cannot be infinite. The first is Aristotle's argument that there must exist an "unmoved mover" to account for motion in the world; the second is the argument that there must exist a first cause; the third that a necessary being must exist; and the fourth that degrees of perfection in the world imply the existence of a supremely perfect being from which partial perfection derives. The fifth argument is the argument from teleology in the inanimate world. Lifeless matter, which cannot itself have a purpose, obeys certain laws and exists in a state of order and direction. This order must have been imposed upon it, and therefore a being which imposes order upon the universe must exist. This proof is similar to the "argument from design", popular in the seventeenth century, which is founded upon an analogy between man-made objects and the universe. When we see an object which "works"—a clock, for example—we know that it must have been made by someone and that it existed in the maker's mind before becoming actual. Similarly, it is argued, when we see that the universe "works", that it follows certain laws, we are bound to assume that it was made by someone, who had in his mind an idea of what he wanted to make. The existence of design in the inanimate world therefore proves the existence of God. This argument is fallacious, because the analogy upon which it is founded is inexact. When we see a clock we know that someone made it only because we have experience of the conditions under which objects such as clocks come into being: we are able to say that clocks belong to the class of manufactured objects. But we do not know how universes come into being: we have no experience of universes as a class, but of only one unique universe. Therefore we are not able to say that universes belong to the class of manufactured objects; therefore the analogy between any particular manufactured object (such as a clock) and the universe is inexact; therefore the argument from design is fallacious. The force of this objection may be more vivid if we imagine that a primitive tribe which has not developed the ability to manufacture machines finds a clock. It has never before seen a clock, or any other mechanical object. Now, this tribe does *not* know the clock was made by someone: it has no means of knowing this, for the clock is something the like of which it has never experienced before. Mankind as a whole is in a comparable situation with respect to the universe.

Thomas' synthesis of Aristotle and Christianity was the high point of Catholic theology of the thirteenth century. During the fourteenth, the synthesis began to be broken down by attacks upon it, chiefly by Franciscans. The greatest of these were John Duns Scotus, who wrote at the turn of the century, and William of Ockham. Duns Scotus, who was born in Scotland about 1265 and died in 1308, possessed one of the most incisive minds of the Middle Ages. He was a convincing critic of traditional and Thomist metaphysics and in general he demanded a more rigorous examination of metaphysical arguments hitherto felt to be satisfactory. Viewed in the perspective of history, he appears as a precursor of Ockhamism, a movement which was chiefly disruptive; but to his own age he was a positive metaphysician who improved the basis of scholastic metaphysics. He acquired a similar authority for the Franciscans as Thomas had for the Dominicans.

William of Ockham (born probably 1280-90, died probably 1349) was the greatest of the schoolmen after Aquinas. (There are two Ockhams in England, one in Yorkshire, one in Surrey: most historians believe William came from the Surrey Ockham). He was a pupil of Duns Scotus, and the leading philosopher of the fourteenth century. He was a complex man and a complex thinker. He can be made to seem very "modern" if his thought is considered out of context. He wanted to sever logic and epistemology from metaphysics and theology, and if one believes his object in this was only to secure the purity and self-sufficiency of logic and epistemology, he seems to be a forerunner of modern philosophy. But he also wanted metaphysics and theology to be purified of unjustified reliance on logic and his object in this was to assert the freedom and omnipotence of God, who was to be shown as above logic. In this direction he is not so "modern".

We have already noticed, when considering Anselm, that

there existed in medieval philosophy a strong tendency to equate the logically true with the objectively real. Some of the strangest ideas of the Middle Ages are a product of this tendency, the cause of which was fundamentally a failure to preserve the distinction between deductive and inductive logic and to understand that analytic propositions can give no factual information about reality. Ockham's achievement as a logician was partly to distinguish analytic propositions from other kinds of propositions and to emphasise their independence of the real world. It was also his work to underline the corollary to this: that inductive arguments founded on empirical observation cannot give certain and necessary truth. He showed that the concept of causation is an empirical concept; that is, the fact that one event causes another event can be established only by experience, and cannot be logically deduced. This meant that the causal argument could not be employed in theology; but it also liberated God from being obliged to conform to the rules of deductive logic. For example, if it is impossible to deduce the existence of A from the existence of B—and this is what the denial of necessary causation means—A and B are distinct entities and God could cause B to exist without A, and A without B. This increases the amount of fredom God is permitted, and in Ockham's theology God is the one absolutely free being. Especially is he free of moral obligation: to Ockham, morality consists in obedience to the will of God and "right" is what God wills. Murder, for example, is wrong, but it is wrong only because God chooses that it should be wrong; it would be possible for him to choose that murder should be right, in which event to commit murder would be meritorious. God himself is not bound by the obligation to be good, for it is he who decides what is good. Ockham was conscious that this is the only logical conclusion to draw from the Christian conception of God, and that the only way of knowing good from evil is through knowing what God has willed shall be good and evil, that is, through revelation.

By means of his purified logic, Ockham showed that supposed

philosophic proofs of Christian dogma were fallacious. He did not seek positively to deny, for example, that the soul was immaterial and immortal, or that man had free will; he sought to show that these "facts" could not be proved by logic, but only believed by faith. To those who considered he had succeeded, it meant the end of the scholastic tradition, which was founded on the faith that the tenets of Christian belief *could* be supported by philosophy. The Ockhamist movement of the fourteenth century was therefore disruptive and, from an orthodox point of view, subversive. Philosophy became separated from theology and no longer lent dogma its support. The possibility of a purely secular philosophy again existed.

William of Ockham was the last great philosopher of the Middle Ages. The followers of Aquinas, Duns Scotus and Ockham shared philosophy between them until the Renaissance of classical learning prepared Europe for the rebirth of philosophical speculation outside the scholastic system.

3   Modern Philosophic Movements

1

THE CLIMATE in which modern philosophy was born was determined by the decline in the power of the church and the rise of empirical science, accompanied by the revival of classical learning. Speculation broke free from subservience to Christian dogma and returned to essentials. The founder of modern philosophy is usually held to be Descartes, and this is certainly true so far as pure speculation is concerned. But, as medieval philosophy was involved with the question of faith, so modern philosophy is characteristically involved with that which replaced faith as the prime concern of Western man : natural and political science; and for the earliest attempts to accommodate philosophy to the discipline of the new sciences we must look to Francis Bacon and to Thomas Hobbes.

Bacon (1561-1626) was concerned to establish scientific method as the sole method for the acquisition of knowledge. Neither the Aristotelean nor the Platonic methods were capable of giving real knowledge about the world, he said, and he proposed a method of induction from observation : one must accumulate data and interpret it. Bacon's proposed method of dealing with this data was peculiar and does not concern us here; and he definitely misunderstood the nature of scientific hypothesis, which must precede the accumulation of data. But his emphasis on the empirical and observational basis of knowledge was the starting-point of the great empirical tradition of British philosophy.

Bacon planned a scientific-philosophical work on a very large scale : nothing less than a grand summary of all knowledge on empirical principles. It was left in a very incomplete state, and his completed work, such as the famous *Essays*, cannot easily be related to it. He was a lawyer by profession and rose to the pinnacle of Lord Chancellor, a post he lost after being convicted of taking bribes. Since all judges in his day took bribes as a normal part of their occupation, we must suppose this to have been a pretext to secure his political fall. The fact that he was notoriously admired but not loved in an age when admiration and love usually went hand in hand should not influence our judgment concerning his intellectual ability. He is the first English philosopher of modern times, and a master of English : since his time, English philosophers have usually felt obliged to be literary artists as well.

Thomas Hobbes (1588-1674) was acquainted with Bacon, but lived on into the period of the Civil War and the Commonwealth, and died at the age of 91 during the last years of the reign of Charles II. Hobbes' scientific opinions were gathered chiefly from Galileo. whom he visited in 1636, his political opinions from the troubled state of England during the 1630s and 1640s. His masterpiece of political philosophy, *Leviathan*, was written during 1650-1, while he was in France as a political refugee.

Hobbes believed he could construct a philosophical explanation of human behaviour on the basis of the science of motion. Human actions, he said, are instances of bodies in motion, and these can be explained by the laws of mechanics. All human motivation, he thought, is either movement towards an object or movement away from an object: the former is called appetite, the latter aversion. Transferred to the public sphere of politics, appetite appears as lust for power, aversion as fear of death. Fundamentally, politics are carried forward by these two forms of motion.

A state, Hobbes taught, is established when men hand over their power to a ruler, the motivation for this act being fear of death in a state of nature. The sole justification for government is the safety of the people, and the sovereign must therefore be absolute, since only if his power is absolute can he protect those he rules. The right of the sovereign to rule derives from the necessity for firm government, and not from God. Cromwell had as much right to absolute power as did Charles I, provided he was capable of exercising it. When Hobbes had made this clear, in *Leviathan*, Cromwell allowed him to return to England. The law is the command of the sovereign: what is lawful is what the sovereign says is lawful. The sovereign is capable of making bad laws, but bad laws are preferable to no laws, because no laws means anarchy, and this is the worst of all conditions, since it leaves men in perpetual fear of death. It is a grave weakness of Hobbes' political philosophy that he can see no mean between absolute rule and anarchy, and seems not to have realised that fear of death from the abuse of absolute power can be as great as fear of death from absence of law. He believed that all men desire power and would ceaselessly strive to satisfy this desire at the expense of others if they were not kept in check by a greater power, that is, by the power of the sovereign. This seems not to be literally true so far as individual men are concerned, since civilisation consists to a large extent in the suppression of aggressive instincts to the point at which they either vanish, and men become docile and to some degree broken, or are sublimated into socially-acceptable expressions; but on a world scale, nations certainly behave as Hobbs said all men would do in the absence of an absolute ruler.

Hobbes is very important as a pioneer of analytic philosophy. He stressed the logical distinction between different classes of words : names, he said, are names of bodies, properties or names, and if one of these classes is used as if it belonged to another class, the result is an absurdity. The problem of universals, he claimed, is a pseudo-problem, the word "universal" being a name for a class of names and not a name for a class of bodies.

Hobbes is impossible to classify because he seems to belong both to the rationalist and to the empiricist traditions. (The exact meaning of these terms will be explained shortly). He sought to explain human behaviour from the laws of motion as then understood, which is a rationalist proceeding and is almost certainly misguided; but in many of his details and in his straightforward, no-nonsense attitude towards problems of knowledge and of ethics he places himself in the empiricist line. Everyone criticises Hobbes, but everyone finds in him something to admire. He is among the most comprehensive thinkers in the history of British philosophy.

2

PROVIDED ONE bears in mind that such a scheme is an extreme simplification, it is possible to describe modern philosophy as two empiricist reactions to rationalism. Classical philosophy from Socrates onwards and modern philosophy from Descartes onwards both differ from medieval philosophy in that they are concerned first and foremost with the powers and limitations of man. In this respect Descartes can be called the modern Socrates. His example led at first to a type of metaphysical thinking termed rationalism. The remoteness from experience of the rationalist systems of his successors Spinoza and Leibniz prompted a reaction, deriving part of its authority from Descartes' contemporary Bacon, which took place in Bacon's homeland, England. The English reaction to continental rationalism is called empiricism. The empirical tradition ceased to be peculiar to England when Kant took it to the continent and claimed to have reconciled it with rationalism in a philosophical synthesis called transcendental idealism. Kant's successors on the continent, especially Hegel and his followers, developed a form of idealism so remote from empiricism as to count as a revived rationalism, and this led in turn to a second English reaction. At the present time, Hegelian idealism is in bad odour everywhere in the West and the empiricist tradition may be said to have triumphed: the contemporary split between positivism in its various forms and existentialism in its various forms is not really a fresh confrontation of rationalism and empiricism, but rather a division between two forms of empiricism.

Let us now be clear exactly what is meant by the philosophical terms "rationalism" and "empiricism". The terms are opposites: the latte consists in a denial of the tenets of the former. Speaking generally, rationalism is the theory that knowledge of the actual world can be attained by a process of pure thinking divorced from experience, empiricism the theory that all knowledge of the actual world is derived from experience. In exact philosophical language (which brings out more vividly the antithetical nature of the two movements), rationalism is the theory that *a priori* concepts provide knowledge of the real world and that synthetic *a priori* propositions are possible, empiricism the denial that *a priori* concepts provide knowledge of the real world and that synthetic *a priori* propositions are possible.

An *a priori* concept is an idea produced by reason or the intellect and not derived from sense-experience. (The opposite of *a priori* is *a posteriori*, meaning "derived from sense experience".) An example of an *a priori* concept is the concept of causality. It is agreed that causality cannot be experienced in the actual world as an event: one cannot see "causality" as one can see a table. The rationalist position in respect of causality is that it is a part of the actual world (i.e. really exists) and since it cannot be experienced, the fact of its existence is discovered by a process of thinking and not of observation: causality is therefore an *a priori* concept which provides knowledge of the real world. The empiricist position is that what is called causality can be reduced to a number of other concepts which are derived from sense experience—i.e. *a posteriori* concepts such as proximity and succession.

The second difference between rationalists and empiricists involves the distinction between analytic and synthetic propositions. An analytic proposition is one whose denial is a contradiction in terms. For example, the proposition "Every effect has a cause" is analytic, because its truth depends upon the meaning of the word "effect", which may be defined as "that which is caused"; to say, therefore, that "Every effect does not have a cause" would be a contradiction in terms. Such a proposition tells us nothing more than the meaning of its own terms: it is tautology. A synthetic proposition, on the other hand, is one which does tell us something more than the meaning of its own terms, and its denial is not a contradiction. For example, the proposition "Every event has a cause" is synthetic, because its truth, if it is true, depends upon observation; the meaning of "event" is not "that which is caused" but "that which occurs", and the proposition "Every event is not caused" may or may not be true but it is not a contradiction in terms. Now, it is obvious that all analytic propositions are *a priori*: that is, their truth does not depend upon sense experience. If we define "effect" as "that which is caused" we do not have to look around us to know that the proposition "Every effect has a cause" is true— its truth follows from the meaning of its terms. The difference between rationalists and empiricists lies in whether any synthetic propositions can ever be *a priori*: that is, whether any proposition which tells us something true about the actual world can contain terms not derived from sense experience. The rationalist view is that synthetic *a priori* propositions exist, and that the propositions of mathematics and the basic facts of physical science are synthetic *a priori* propositions. The general empiricist view is that the concepts of logic and mathematics are indeed *a priori*, but that therefore the propositions in which they occur are analytic and do not define anything except their own terms. The facts of science and the actual world, however, derive from observation, and the propositions in which they occur must all be synthetic *a posteriori* : synthetic *a priori* knowledge is therefore impossible.

The propositions of mathematics are those which throw the difficulty of this problem into the highest relief. Consider the proposition "7 + 5 = 12". Is it analytic or synthetic? The pure rationalist view is that it is a synthetic *a priori* proposition : that is, it is a proposition whose truth does not depend upon sense perception but which tells us a true fact about the actual world. The pure empiricist view is that, since it does tell us something about the actual world, it must be synthetic *a posteriori*, that is, its truth must depend upon sense experience. Among the empiricist philosophers, however, only J. S. Mill ventured to draw this extreme conclusion, which implies that further experience might contradict the proposition "7 + 5 = 12". Hume, for example, felt obliged to say that such propositions were analytic, but this is hardly more satisfactory, since an analytic proposition is one which tells us only about the meaning of its own terms, and it cannot with plausibility be denied that "7 + 5 = 12" does tell us something about the real world. Kant attempted, within the context of his own philosophy, to resolve this difficulty by saying that mathematical propositions are synthetic *a priori* and then giving synthetic *a priori* propositions a special status.

3

THE THREE great rationalist philosophers are Descartes, Spinoza and Leibniz. Réné Descartes (1596-1650), known as the founder of modern philosophy, was the author of the first great philosophical work in French, the *Discourse on Method* (1637), which, with the *Meditations on the First Philosophy* (1641), is the principal source of his opinions. Descartes was attracted early to mathematics, in which he found a system of certain knowledge absent from all other studies; and he came to think that the world must be capable of being understood by the same methods as mathematical axioms are understood. His desire was, put rather crudely, to rewrite philosophy as if it were mathematics, building a body of knowledge on the basis of some indubitable axiom. This determination of Descartes to remake philosophy in the image of mathematics was the seed of philosophical rationalism.

His initial task was to discover if any basic—or, as he put it, indubitable—axiom existed, and to discover it he resolved to doubt everything that could be doubted. By proceeding methodically, he found he could doubt the truth of everything except the fact that he was doubting—and since doubt was a kind of thinking, the fact that he was thinking. One indubitable axiom therefore existed: *cogito, ergo sum*—I am thinking, therefore I am. From this axiom he proceeds to construct a philosophy. He can remove from himself every attribute except thought, therefore he is a being whose essence, or essential attribute, is to think. The content of his thought includes the idea of a perfect being which, for reasons that do not now seem compelling and include the ontological argument, he concludes must exist outside his thought. The existence of God, which Descartes now regards as proved, re-establishes many of the commonsense ideas which he had found it necessary initially to doubt—for, he argues, a perfect being would not allow us to be systematically and fundamentally deceived about the nature of our world: the reality of physical objects is reasserted. The most important physical object (to us) is our body, and the most difficult problem we now have to face is how the thinking part of us (or soul) is united with the physical part of us (or body). Descartes' solution is that there are two and only two substances or existants in the world of created things: "thinking" substances, or soul, and "extended" substances, or matter. Reality cannot be reduced further than this, for the mechanistic laws which, in common with other 17th century scientists, he believed governed the operations of nature, cannot be applied to the non-material or "thinking" substance. Thus the search for a basic unity is abandoned, and a duality is substituted. The essence of matter is extension, as the essence of the soul is thought: the idea of extension is an "innate" or *a priori* idea. But how the two sole substances, whose essences exclude one another, are united, Descartes is unable to say.

On the basis of a small number of *a priori* concepts—the axioms of mathematics; the "cogito" and the concept of extension, involving the concept of two basic substances; and the idea of God—Descartes thought he could construct the principles of a single, united science or Tree of Knowledge, of which the roots would be metaphysics, the trunk physics, and the branches all the other sciences. Perhaps this image of all knowledge evolving axiomatically from metaphysics gives a clearer idea than any explanation of what is meant by "rationalism" in philosophy.

It must not be supposed that a completely "secular" approach to the fundamental problems of life such as Descartes inaugurated was received with equinimity by the Church. Although he professed to be an orthodox Catholic, Descartes was considered hopelessly heretical, and the *Discourse* and the *Meditations* went on to the Index. He was compelled to leave France and settle in Holland, but Dutch Protestantism ultimately found him as unsettling as French Catholicism, and he spent his last year in Sweden. Twenty years after his death, the teaching of his philosophy was forbidden in all French universities.

Benedict de Spinoza (1632-1677) was a Spanish Jew born in Amsterdam of parents who had fled there from persecution. As a consequence of his unorthodoxy he was excommunicated from the Jewish community and cursed in a document as repellent as anything to come out of the Vatican—a reminder that it has not been only Christian philosophers who have had to contend with the cry of "heresy". He lived by grinding and polishing lenses and pursued his studies at night. With no advantage but his own genius, he became the centre of a circle of intellectual and scientific leaders of the time. His philosophy he said, had no other object than to discover how men might live happily. The beauty of his temperament shines through all he wrote and all he did.

His chief book, the *Ethics*, is one of the classic works of philosophy, and one of the most difficult. It is rationalist in the most rigorous sense of the word: from a number of definitions, axioms and theorems he sets out to prove metaphysical and ethical truths after the manner of Euclidean proofs of geometrical theorems. Spinoza's starting-point, in the *Ethics*, is Descartes' unsolved problem of the duality of soul and matter. Spinoza denies that these are a real duality. This is a mistake caused by supposing they are both substances, but there is in reality only one substance or being, which is God. God is all and everything, infinite in every respect. He has an infinite number of modes of being, but of these we know only two: thought and extension. Difficulty arises only if we imagine that thought and extension are substances, for then it would be impossible to explain how they are united in man. In reality, however, the difficulty does not exist, since both are modes of one basic substance or being. The natural sciences study being in the mode of extension, and Spinoza intends to study it in the mode of thought: human actions will be considered in the same way as lines, planes or bodies are considered. The implication of all this is a complete pantheism and an absolute determinism: the world is as it is by *logical* necessity— this is of the essence of rationalism—and free will is therefore impossible. But this does not mean that happiness is impossible: happiness is attained through understanding how human life is integrated in the grand design and accepting the necessity of all events. When one knows the cause of an event one accepts the event as inevitable and relinquishes the delusion that men act as they do because they have some "purpose". Hatred and resentment are inappropriate reactions to the behaviour of others, to the state of the world, and to the nature of God. Since he is infinite in power and knowledge, God has created everything of which an infinite intellect is capable of conceiving; therefore he is beyond good and evil, having created both good and evil things as parts of a whole embodying every possible form of existence.

Spinoza's philosophy is very like that of the Stoics, and the contradiction between the deterministic metaphysics and the ethical teachings which we noted in the Stoic philosophy is apparent in his. But this notwithstanding, Spinoza's system is the most impressive rationalist structure ever constructed, and its contemporary importance lies in its having taken the rationalist position to an extreme: if even Spinoza failed, one may think, then the rationalist endeavour as such is perhaps doomed to failure.

Viewed in retrospect, the climax of rationalist thinking about the physical world came with the philosophy of Gottfried Wilhelm Leibniz (1646-1716), but in his own day Leibniz was little appreciated. The works he published were of the popular variety designed to please his readers, and his best-known dictum was that this is the best of all possible worlds, a conclusion following from God's infinite power combined with his infinite goodness. Mockery of this dictum forms the basis of Voltaire's famous satire *Candide*, in which Leibniz appears as Dr. Pangloss. The Pangloss parody of Leibniz and, by implication, of philosophers in general, is of course unfair to Leibniz's truly enormous intellect, but it does give permanent form to an objection to the rationalist philosophers which it would be unphilosophical to repudiate. Through an immense effort of intellect and the acquisition of great learning, philosophers were arriving at conclusions which seemed to be completely untrue and in some respects fantastic. To a witty commentator like Voltaire, this seemed merely comic; it took other philosophers to see what might actually be going wrong—namely, that the attempt to raise a comprehensive science of life on the basis of a few *a priori* concepts was misguided.

By a process of reasoning, Leibniz decided that all previous and contemporary descriptions of substance, atoms, space, time and matter were inadequate, and that the only possible element must be an unextended substance which was a bearer of energy : this simple substance he called a monad. Monads can be created and annihilated but cannot otherwise be changed. No monad can effect another monad, so there is no causation. As a monad has no extension, it does not exist in space or time, and contains no matter. The essence of a monad is activity, and all monads are therefore alike. It follows from all this that the observed variety of the spatio-temporal world can be produced by only one means : varying degrees of activity in monads. The least active monads are "matter", the one completely active monad is God. The form of activity carried on by monads is the perceiving or mirroring of other monads : the more active the monad, the more clearly it mirrors. The less active monads produce the appearance of the material world, although in reality there is no material, only monads. The union of soul and body is a case of mirroring : the soul and body appear to interact, but in reality they may be compared with two synchronised clocks or two choirs singing from the same score.

Space and time are not empirical realities but appearances : space is the order of existences which are possible simultaneously, time the order of possible existences which are inconsistent with one another. Every monad has a degree of activity different from that of every other monad, but these degrees are infinitely small : thus the monads form an infinite series, from the least to the most active. This series of compossible monads is "space". But the state of each monad is not constant : it exists in a series of successive states which unfold in pre-established harmony with the unfolding of the successive states of every other monad. This series of successive states is "time". The universe is a plenum formed of these two series.

It is not necessary to pursue Leibniz's metaphysical system any further to understand what it essentially is : a description of the actual world as if it were a series of logical propositions. By thinking about the demands of logic, Leibniz believed he could discover the facts of the actual world. The outlandish result is a first-rate example of what made empiricism a pressing necessity for the future development of philosophy.

4

THE GREAT empiricists whose work was a response and counterweight to continental rationalism were Locke, in the seventeenth century, and Berkeley and Hume in the eighteenth. Until our own times, Hume was universally accepted as undoubtedly the greatest English-speaking philosopher. (Today the palm would probably go to Bertrand Russell).

John Locke (1632-1704) was born in Wrington, Somerset. His chief work, the *Essay concerning Human Understanding,* written over a period of nearly 20 years, was published in 1690, two years after the Glorious Revolution of 1688, of which he was partly the inspirer. One should not be misled by the modest title: the *Essay* is in fact a very large work and one of the classics of epistemology. Locke's fundamental outlook contrasts vividly with the views we have just been considering. It may be summarised as empirical, scientific and commonsense. The physical world, he says, is what physicists say it is: material bodies composed of particles. These bodies operate like machines, and to all intents and purposes are machines. In addition to material bodies there are evidently immaterial substances which act through sense organs. When sense organs are stimulated there are produced in the brain two kinds of "ideas"—"ideas of sensation", which are those directly acquired from outside, and "ideas of reflection", which are produced by the mind through operating upon the ideas received from outside. These two kinds of ideas constitute the whole of consciousness and thought; consequently we can have nothing in our minds that has not been provided by experience. How the stimulation of sense organs produces ideas in the mind Locke does not pretend to know; but that it does so, and that this is the sole origin of ideas, seems to him self-evident. It follows that all we are immediately aware of is the ideas in our own minds, and that "knowledge" consists in perceiving the connections between ideas.

Politically, Locke was the philosopher of limited monarchy and so of the revolution of 1688. His *Two Treatises of Government* were published in the same year as the *Essay*: the first refutes the theory of absolutist government, the second states his own political theory. Unfortunately for ease of study, this theory is not the antithesis of Hobbes' theory of absolutism, and, again unfortunately, Locke's account of how the state came into existence through a "contract" between ruler and ruled is certainly false. Like Hobbes, Locke believed that a sovereign was necessary for government, but unlike Hobbes he refused to allow the sovereign absolute authority. He must be held to account for his actions, and the proper body to hold him to account was an assembly in some sense representative of the people. This is not "democracy"— for the people do not rule—it is "limited monarchy" of precisely the kind instituted by the 1688 revolution. Much of what is loosely called "democracy" is in reality Lockean limited monarchy. It would be easy, for example, to view the actual government of the United States in this light, with the president as monarch (during his term of office) and congress as the assembly which limits his powers. France under de Gaulle was a *de facto* limited monarchy.

Locke's political and epistemological views were exactly in accord with the spirit of his age, and· it is to this fact, rather than to any startling originality, that they owed their prestige. Scientific materialism was in the ascendant, and Locke gave it philosophical expression. It followed therefore that to a man so out of tune with the spirit of the age as George Berkeley, Locke must seem abhorrent; and a drive to refute Locke was the initial impulse which led Berkeley to philosophise.

Born in 1685 near Kilkenny, Ireland, Berkeley was Bishop of Cloyne from 1734 to his death in 1753. He read Locke's *Essay* while still a young man and was appalled both by it and by its universal acceptance. As a religious man he detested Locke's materialism, which seemed to him to be destructive of faith in

God, and considered his theory that the mind knows only the ideas produced within it contrary to commonsense. For, he argued, if the mind knows nothing but its own ideas, how can it know that the objects it thinks it perceives in the material world actually exist? This objection to Locke's theory of knowledge had already occurred to others, and Berkeley had a very radical solution for it. If, as Locke argued, the mind was conscious only of its own ideas, what need was there for the material world at all? The difficulties in Locke's philosophy arose from supposing that there existed two substances, the material and the mental—that a table, for instance, was both a collection of material particles and a collection of mental ideas—and then saying that all the mind could know was the ideas: for if this were so, what reason was there for supposing the material substances had any distinct existence? None whatever. Abolish the material substance, and nothing is changed: the world is still as it was. This, then, is what Berkeley proceeded to do: he denied the existence of matter, and maintained that the actual world was a creation of the mind.

For an object to exist, it must be perceived. If it were not perceived, it would not exist. Does this mean that objects cease to exist when no one is perceiving them, and jump back into existence when they again become objects of perception? No, because God perceives all things all the time, If our ideas are not produced by some object corresponding to them in some way, how are they produced? God inserts them directly into our minds. Berkeley found an ingenious answer to every objection raised to his abolition of matter; but ingenuity is not enough to make so fantastic an idea really credible, and no one (except Berkeley himself, presumably) has ever supposed it to be. Yet to dismiss Berkeley as a famous crank is to be too hasty. Although in his desire to prove the non-existence of matter he distorted it, he had got hold of a concept of first-rate importance: the concept of sense-data. A sense-datum is the immediate object of sense perception—that which one is actually conscious of perceiving. The sense-data of an hallucination are as "genuine" as the sense-data of the perception of real objects; the sense-data of the perception of real objects are as private as the sense-data of an hallucination. Berkeley expressed his theory that matter is mental by saying in effect that material objects constitute private sense-data. (He uses the term "idea", which proves to be too imprecise; but the description he gives of "ideas" shows that he means what are now called "sense-data".)

The empiricist line of Locke and Berkeley was completed by David Hume (1711-1776), a Scotsman. His importance lies supremely in the field of epistemology, presented in his *Treatise of Human Nature* and the shorter *Inquiry into Human Understanding*, and the heart of his epistemological theory is the sceptical doctrine that there are severe limits to what we really know.

Hume says that the content of the mind is composed of what he calls impressions and ideas. Impressions are derived from sense experience, ideas are more or less distinct images of impressions formed in thinking and reasoning. Every simple idea corresponds to a simple impression; and we can have no distinct idea of anything of which we have received no impression. This means that any idea purporting to be of something not perceived is either void of content or can be reduced to simple perceptions. The "self", for example, says Hume, is not perceived, and so it cannot be part of knowledge except as a collection of other perceptions which do not add up to a distinct notion of "self".

All certain knowledge is either deductive or empirical, empirical knowledge being impressions and the ideas which are the images of impressions. Inductive knowledge from empirical data is only probable knowledge. Thus there are many things which in the ordinary way we think we know which we do not know for certain. Causation is one. We can perceive that A is bigger than B, or that it is on top of B, but we cannot perceive that A causes B. Causation is the principle which we suppose links separate events together and by which we are led to expect the existence of one object or event from the prior existence of some other object or event. But causation is really only the observed fact that A is invariably accompanied by B, which leads to the expectation that it will always be accompanied by B. This expectation, however, cannot be justified by the only two certain ways of obtaining knowledge, that is, deductively or empirically. There is, in fact, no rational justification for thinking that what has been conjoined in the past will be conjoined in the future. The supposition that the future resembles the past is not founded on argument but is entirely a matter of habit.

All probable reasoning follows taste and sentiment. There is no abstract justification for preferring one principle to another. If we do prefer one, it is because we like it more. This sceptical doubt concerning the validity of all non-deductive reasoning Hume calls a "malady" from which one can free oneself only by "carelessness and inattention": one can live happily only by forgetting what one knows. So far as he can see, the sole reason for studying philosophy is that one likes to do it: that, at any rate, is the reason *he* does it.

Hume's conclusion is that "empiricism" teaches nothing about the world, but that there is no other way to knowledge of the world. This conclusion seems disastrous, and it will be clear that whoever followed Hume would be obliged either to refute him or in some way circumvent him. The latter course was that taken by the next great philosopher of the West, Immanuel Kant.

It is sometimes said that the term "British" has no real meaning if one is describing a type of man, but that individual men are English or Scottish or Irish or Welsh. The history of British philosophy offers evidence against this view. Locke was English, Berkeley Irish, Hume Scottish—yet all three were undoubtedly "British" when they wrote philosophy. That is, they all belonged to the same instinctive school—for of course no actual "school" existed—and none of them could possibly be mistaken for a French, German or Greek philosopher. They were all masters of the art of writing, like Bacon and Hobbes before them and Bradley and Russell after them, and like these they were keenly interested in social and political affairs.

David Hume was a many-sided man. As an historian he shares with Gibbon the distinction of having freed the writing of history from ecclesiastical bias. He was one of the few philosophers to have made a point of his unbelief and he wrote a famous essay on the impossibility of miracles. His fame in his own day rested chiefly on his "atheism". He spent many years in Paris at the British embassy, where he was for a time lionised by society and made easy sexual conquests, for he was, according to all the evidence, very attractive to women. The conception of the philosopher as a dessicated thinking machine of repellent aspect is a libel on all but a few of the great philosophers and patently absurd in the case of Hume, one of the very greatest.

Empirical epistemology had its counterpart in the empirical theory of ethics called utilitarianism, which judges as good that which contributes in the greatest measure to human happiness. The founder of utilitarianism was Jeremy Bentham (1748-1832), who was also famous as a leading reformer in the legal, economic and educational fields. As a political and a humanising influence in eighteenth century Europe, Bentham is of first-rate importance, but as a philosopher his importance has been diminished by his rather shallow psychology. The only principles upon which men act, says Bentham, are the drive to acquire pleasure and the drive to avoid pain. The moral worth of an action is to be judged according to whether it tends to increase the happiness or pleasure of those affected by it. If the whole community is affected, then the principle of "the greatest good of the greatest number" is the principle to apply. The philosophy of utility was developed by John Stuart Mill (1806-1873), the chief English radical of his age. He became a Benthamite at the age of 15 (Mill was extremely precocious), and for ever after applied the test of utility to all philosophical and economic and political questions. In Mill, empiricism was complete. He denied the existence of "innate" ideas and moral intuition and considered that deductive reasoning was purely mental and that any proposition which gave information about the real world must be synthetic. Even the propositions of mathematics—e.g. "$7+5=12$"—were, he thought, inductive propositions, that is, no more than well-founded generalisations from experience. The fundamental ethical doctrine of *Utilitarianism*, Mill's ethical work, is a reassertion of Bentham's principle of the greatest good of the greatest number.

5

KANT (1724-1804) is widely accorded the status of the greatest modern philosopher. His system, which he called the critical philosophy or transcendental idealism, is central to modern philosophy and was the starting-point of most philosophy of the nineteenth century. How far his system may still be considered valid is a matter for debate (later knowledge has certainly invalidated it in some respects) but that he was a very great thinker cannot possibly be doubted. A study of his philosophy which included a study of the problems he inherited and of the movements to which he later gave rise would almost constitute a study of modern philosophy in general. Only the briefest outline is possible here.

Kant proposes to undertake a synthesis of rationalism and empiricism. He begins with an examination of the propositions of logic as it was understood in his day. These propositions— or, as Kant calls them, judgments—he classifies as either analytic or synthetic, and either *a priori* or *a posteriori*. An analytic judgment is one whose predicate is contained in its subject and the denial of which is therefore a self-contradiction. For example, the judgment "All triangles have three sides" is analytic, because the predicate "three sides" is contained in the subject "triangle", which means a three-sided figure; thus its denial is a self-contradiction. A synthetic judgment is one whose predicate is not contained in its subject and the denial of which is not a self-contradiction. For example, the judgment "Alcohol is a soporific" is synthetic, because the predicate "soporific" is not contained in the subject "alcohol" and the judgment can be denied without self-contradiction (i.e. to say

"Alcohol is not a soporific" may or may not be true, but is not self-contradictory). An *a priori* judgment is one which is independent of experience. For example, the judgment "The good go to Heaven when they die" is perhaps true and perhaps false, but is not verifiable or refutable by experience: therefore it is either without meaning or *a priori*. An *a posteriori* judgment is one which does depend upon experience. For example, the judgment "Oranges are sweet" can be verified or refuted by experience, i.e. by tasting oranges.

On the basis of these distinctions, Kant classifies judgments as being of three possible kinds: analytic *a priori*, synthetic *a posteriori* and synthetic *a priori*. An example of a synthetic *a priori* judgment (in Kant's opinion) is "Every event has a cause". It is synthetic because its predicate "cause" is not contained in its subject "event" and its denial is not self-contradictory. It is *a priori* because it is not verifiable by experience. The judgments of mathematics, science and morality are, he maintains, synthetic *a priori*. And he is then concerned to discover how they are possible.

Following the psychology of his age, Kant divides the mind into two parts: the part which perceives and the part which thinks. The perceiving mind is the recipient of the impressions of the senses, and the impressions it receives are called "particulars". The thinking mind is the organ of understanding, and the objects of the understanding are called "concepts". The application of concepts to particulars constitutes synthetic judgments.

Kant defines three types of concept: the concept which is abstracted from sense perception and is applied to it, which he calls *a posteriori*; the concept which is applicable to sense perception but is not abstracted from it, which he calls *a priori*; and the concept which is neither abstracted from sense perception nor applicable to it, which he calls an Idea. *A posteriori* concepts are familiar to us from the empiricists and constitute ordinary empirical concepts. Kant's individual philosophy begins with his consideration of *a priori* concepts.

He maintains, firstly, that the propositions of arithmetic

and geometry are both synthetic and *a priori*—that is to say, that arithmetical and geometrical concepts are concepts applied to particulars which are not objects of sense-perception, i.e. to *a priori* particulars. These *a priori* particulars are time and space. The propositions of arithmetic describe the structure of time, those of geometry the structure of space. The concepts of mathematics are *a priori* concepts describing time and space, which are *a priori* particulars.

The concepts of science and everyday knowledge which are *a priori*—that is. concepts applied to sense perception but not abstracted from it—Kant calls "categories". For example, the judgment that an event is caused by some other event does not derive from sense perception, since we cannot perceive causation, but it is applied to sense perception, and it is therefore a synthetic *a priori* judgment. The concept "A causes B" is an *a priori* concept applied to perception. Kant therefore calls the concept of causation a category. From each of the different logical forms of judgment Kant derives a table of twelve categories. These categories are arranged in four groups of three: categories of quantity, of quality, of relation and of modality. The categories of quantity are unity, plurality and totality; of quality reality, negation and limitation; of relation substance-and-accident, causality-and-dependence and community or interaction; of modality possibility-impossibility, existence-non-existence and necessity-contingency. Synthetic *a priori* judgments consist in applying the categories to the perceptions of sense in time and space. Sense perception ordered in time and space is called the perceptual manifold. The categories are not derived from the manifold, but imposed upon it, and it is through them that what would otherwise be disconnected sensations becomes part of the systematically connected objective world we are conscious of. The imposition of the categories upon the perceptual manifold is called "thinking". That which is capable of being characterised by the categories is called an "object". And the operation of thinking upon objects is what we mean by "objective reality".

In forming this conception, Kant compared himself to

Copernicus: as Copernicus had made the stars stand still and the observer move, instead of the other way round, so he had made the objects conform to the observer's concepts instead of the observer's concepts conforming to the objects. To be apprehensible, an object must conform to the categories. If an object cannot conform to them, it cannot exist for a human observer.

From the existence of the categories, Kant deduces the existence of "things-in-themselves". To "know" a thing is both to perceive it and to think it. What we can think of but cannot perceive, we cannot "know". Now, we are bound to think that the objects we perceive in space and time and under the forms of the categories must have some existence outside those forms in order that the forms may be imposed upon them. And the object "as it is" Kant calls the "thing-in-itself". In alternative phraseology, he calls the object as it is perceived the "phenomenon", and the object as it is in itself the "noumenon". The world as perceived he calls the phenomenal world, the world as it is in itself, the nounmenal world.

It is part of Kant's critique of metaphysics to say that the application of the categories to things-in-themselves produces error and illusion.

The third type of concept distinguished by Kant is the Ideas —concepts which are neither derived from sense perception nor applicable to it. As he had deduced the twelve categories from the different logical forms of judgment, so he deduces the three Ideas from the different forms of logical inference, which, he says, demand ultimately three kinds of absolute unity. The first is the absolute unity of the thinking subject, and the Idea of this is the subject-matter of speculative psychology. The second is the absolute unity of the sequence of the conditions of the appearance, and the Idea of this is the subject-matter of speculative cosmology. The third is the absolute unity of the condition of objects of thought in general, and the Idea of this is the subject-matter of speculative theology. But these three kinds of absolute unity can never be experienced, and the Ideas deriving from them are therefore, as Kant puts it, transcendental: they cannot correspond to any object of experience. The faculty of employing the transcendental Ideas is "reason". Although they do not apply to anything perceived, without them reasoning would lack direction. The Ideas of the soul, of the world as a totality, and of God—which are the three forms of absolute unity demanded by the three forms of logical inference—can never be objects of experience, but pure reason demands them as concepts. But if these concepts are applied to supposed objects of experience—as if they were *a posteriori* concepts or categories—then error and illusion results.

The propositions of metaphysics are without meaning if they involve either the application of the categories to things-in-themselves or the application of the Ideas to experienced reality.

The foregoing is expounded in the *Critique of Pure Reason*, Kant's masterpiece. In the *Critique of Practical Reason*, he is concerned with the synthetic *a priori* principles of morality. To be moral, he says, a man's actions must conform to the "moral law", and that law, which he calls the categorical imperative, states that an action is moral if the performer of the action can will that it should become a universal law. This moral law is formal. That is to say, an action is moral if the maxim upon which it is based can be made into a universal law without contradiction. It is immoral when a contradiction would result if its maxim were universalised. We shall see what the categorical imperative means if we apply it to some specific act—the act of lying, for example. A man who tells a lie acts upon the implied maxim: "In the circumstances under which I say what I know to be untrue, I ought to say what I know to be untrue". If this maxim is made a universal law, it becomes: "Whenever the circumstances under which I say what I know to be untrue obtain, everyone ought to say what he knows to be untrue". But this maxim is self-defeating, since the object of lying is to be believed, and one will not be believed if it is a universal law that, in the circumstances under which one is lying, everyone ought to lie. To lie is therefore immoral—not because one does not like being lied to, or because one feels guilty at telling a lie, but because the maxim upon which a liar acts cannot become a universal law without self-contradiction.

Obedience to the categorical imperative constitutes "duty", and an act is moral, not with reference to the desires of the performer or the effect of the act, but to whether or not it is in accordance with duty.

Kant's third critique, the *Critique of Judgment*, is concerned with subjective teleological and aesthetic principles. The ascription of purpose to nature, says Kant, is part of all scientific explanation. But purpose is not a category, it is a method of ordering our reasoning about nature—that is, a concept of pure reason, or an Idea. Because our reasoning faculties are as they are, we need the concept of purpose. But since this concept is subjective it cannot be applied to objective reality. Aesthetic judgments are similarly subjective. The ascription of purpose to nature is the Idea of a harmony of its parts directed to some specific end, and the ascription of beauty to some object is also the Idea of a harmony of its parts—a purposiveness perceived apart from the presentation of a purpose.

Kant was much more the popular idea of what a philosopher is like than the British empiricists were. He lived entirely for philosophy, teaching it, writing it, thinking it. He never left his native city of Koenigsberg his whole life long: he found all the experience he needed in books and his own brain. This is not to say that he failed to take a lively interest in world affairs and the politics of his time, but he took it from a distance. Politically he was liberal, advocated a "league of nations" and welcomed the French Revolution as a liberating force. But the example of his life exerted more influence than his opinions in these matters, and on the whole it was a bad example: Kant set the pattern for generations of German philosophers and intellectuals who were content to live out their lives in studious seclusion and leave the running of the world to the "authorities". To grasp how completely the intellectuals of Germany divorced themselves from the organising of the nation is to understand a great deal about Germany's political history. Kant provided a bad example, too, in the matter of style. When he wrote essays which he obviously considered of minor importance he wrote in a clear, plain style, but his great philosophical works are couched in involved, opaque language which makes them difficult to read, quite apart from the inherent difficulty of the subject-matter. This excessive obscurity—bad writing, in fact—became after Kant a mark of German philosophical writings and it sometimes degenerated into a repellent jargon incomprehensible to the non-specialist. Philosophers were accused of deliberately writing in this way so as *not* to be understood by non-philosophers, and there is some truth in the charge. Philosophy and elegance of style are by no means incompatible, as Plato showed long ago. Kant may, and indeed must, be forgiven what was no more than an idiosyncracy, but one is not obliged to extend this forgiveness to lesser men who have permitted themselves to write badly because Kant wrote badly.

Kant's influence has been very widespread, but the synthesis of rationalism and empiricism achieved in his philosophy did not prove to be enduring. The weak point at which they split asunder again was the dichotomy established by Kant between the known world of phenomena and the unknowable world of things-in-themselves. He distinguished two kinds of philosopical idealism: dogmatic and transcendental. Idealism, in its philosophical usage, means the doctrine that the objective world can have no reality apart from the mind which perceives it. This means that we have knowledge only of minds and sense experience, and this Kant called dogmatic idealism. In his own philosophy he claimed to have shown that the mind imposes upon the world a structure to which objects must conform. That which cannot conform to this structure transcends experience. Consequently, objects as they are in themselves— that is , apart from the perceiving mind—transcend experience, and this he called transcendental idealism. The dominant move- ment in German philosophy after Kant rejected the "thing-in- itself" on the ground that, on Kant's admission, it was totally unknowable, and if unknowable no conceivable part of human experience. This movement returned to dogmatic idealism—that is, it admitted the existence of mind and sense experience alone. But because of the way in which it developed it is described by a third term: absolute idealism.

6

KANT'S IMMEDIATE successor was Johann Gottlieb Fichte (1762-1814). It will be remembered that Berkeley had claimed that the material world was a product of the mind, and when called upon to account for the origin of the ideas present in the mind had said that they were placed there by God. This form of "idealism" is consistent only with an unquestioning (and unphilosophical) belief in the existence and goodness of God. Kant had concluded that the existence of God was not demonstrable (although there was room for faith in his existence) and it was not necessary to postulate him to account for the observed world, which had its origin in the things-in-themselves. Fichte rejected the thing-in-itself on the ground that it was, according to Kant, unknowable, and was led into asserting that the mind creates, not only the categories and the *a priori* particulars space and time, but also the perceptual manifold. This view seems quite unreasonable, and was in fact soon superseded by the philosophically more satisfactory and historically far more influential form of idealism associated above all with Hegel.

Georg Wilhelm Friedrich Hegel (1770-1831) was the most potent philosophical influence of the nineteenth century. His writings are difficult to understand and what became famous as the Hegelian philosophy is a simplified and in some respects distorted version of what he himself taught. The reaction against him was also in some ways a reaction against the distorted and not the real Hegel. The most influential part of Hegel's philosophy is his dialectic—that is, his own peculiar form of logic.

Hegel's dialectic originated in Kant's classification of the categories. It will be remembered that, according to Kant, there are twelve categories which can be arranged in four groups of three, and Kant remarks that the third category in each group arises from a connection of the first and second of its group: thus, to take the three categories of quantity—unity, plurality and totality—the category totality arises from a connection of unity and plurality, and is in fact plurality regarded as unity. This is Hegel's dialectic in a nutshell. Unity is, in Hegelian terminology, the "thesis", plurality the "antithesis", and totality the "synthesis" of a dialectical unit. By means of this triadic dialectic Hegel undertakes to show how the highest forms of the spirit (or mind in an all-embracing sense) can be logically deduced on *a priori* principles. He begins with the most general statement possible about the universe: that it is. "The universe is being" is the thesis of this initial dialectical step. But this statement is clearly inadequate as a description of the universe, since about being as such, without predicates, one can say and know nothing. This leads us to the antithesis: "The universe is nothing". But this is equally unsatisfactory, since if we cannot know anything about being we certainly cannot know anything about nothing. Consequently, we take the third step of combining thesis and antithesis to produce a synthesis of being and nothing, which is becoming: "The universe is becoming". It ought not to be asserted that Hegel's logic proceeds entirely by this three-step process, but what is characteristic of it is founded upon the idea demonstrated in the above-quoted dialectical unit: the idea that any description is in some measure inadequate; that its opposite corrects what is inadequate, but is itself inadequate; and that a synthesis of these two opposing descriptions is nearer to the truth. This synthesis, however, is also inadequate and when one discovers its opposite one has created a new thesis and antithesis from the combination of which one produces a new synthesis. By this continuing process, Hegel claimed to be able to deduce logically the nature of reality—that is, to produce a description of it incapable of further logical development on dialectical lines. This final term is called the "Absolue Idea", and the steps by which it is reached constitute its progressive logical unfolding. Hegel's definition of the Absolute Idea as unity of the subjective and objective is that it is a concept whose object, which is the Idea, is itself; in other words, thought whose object is thought. (There is a clear similarity between this and Aristotle's God.)

The dialectic here outlined would have perhaps been of interest to philosophers only had Hegel not maintained that its process could be applied to the activites of men and to the historical development of civilisation. In his very impressive *Encyclopaedia of the Philosophical Sciences* he attempts a comprehensive account of his system as applied to reason, to nature and to man. Its tripartite division, while not literally reducible to thesis-antithesis-synthesis, is obviously suggested by, and calculated to suggest, a three-step process. The first part is a summary of his logic (i.e. of the dialectic); the second part constitutes his philosophy of nature; and the third part his philosophy of spirit (or mind). The philosophy of nature is divided into three parts: mechanics, physics and organics. The philosophy of spirit is also divided into three parts: subjective spirit, objective spirit and absolute spirit; and these three parts are further divided into three sub-parts: subjective spirit comprises anthropology, the phenomenology of the spirit (i.e. the forms in which the spirit actualises itself) and psychology; objective spirit comprises right (or justice), morality and ethics; and absolute spirit comprises art, religion and philosophy. It will be noticed that philosophy is thus the supreme activity of man—a conclusion which did much to foster Hegel's popularity among teachers of the subject.

The logic had already been expounded in Hegel's *Science of Logic*; the philosophy of objective spirit is elaborated in his *Philosophy of Right* and his lectures on the philosophy of history; and the philosophy of absolute spirit is developed in his lectures on art, religion and the history of philosophy. The groundwork of his system is laid in his first book, *The Phenomenology of the Spirit*. Taken as a whole it represents one of the most tremendous sustained attempts to comprehend reality ever made. But it is also a reassertion of what can loosely be called philosophical rationalism. and its inflluence has been strongest at just the point at which philosophical rationalism is weak: in its claim to deduce from logical constructions the nature of the actual world. The dialectic is employed to give an account of the historical development of philosophy, and it is useful if the object is simplification and broad generalisation (the reader will notice that the present account of modern philosophical movements is in this dialectical form). It has to be very much modified when one enters into detail. As a philosophical account of the development of history it has had great practical influence. Broadly speaking, Hegel claimed to have discovered that the "world spirit" reveals itself progressively in the actual world through the development of succeeding civilisations, and that this development can be expressed in dialectical form. This means that one can speak of the "world process" (or, more crudely, of "the march of history") and can consciously put oneself in rapport with this process ("be on the side of history"). Two apparently contradictory attitudes are the logical outcome of this view. One, which was that adopted by Hegel himself, is an extreme conservatism amounting to enthusiastic appioval of the existing state of affairs and worship of political success as such (for if the dialectic is right, what is later must be better). The other is an extreme radicalism amounting to enthusiasm for any revolutionary activity which has as its object the elimination of the existing order provided it seems to have a good chance of success (for if the dialectic is right, what is later still must be better still). This latter view stands behind the kind of philosophic anarchism espoused by Michael Bakunin, which is, historically speaking, of little importance; but it is also the inspiration of Marxism, in so far as that doctrine is a philosophy of history.

7

THE PHILOSOPHY of Karl Marx (1818-1883) is called (although not by him) "dialectical materialism". The materialist part of it derives ultimately from the materialism of the eighteenth century, of which the philosophy of Locke is a good English example: to Locke and to Marx, man is principally a material object. Marx adds that the distinguishing characteristic of man is that he is able to invent tools, and the development of technology determines the development of society: men are what they are *in every respect* as a consequence of how they organise the work they have to do. Mental life is determined by physical and social needs, and the institutions and ideas to which mental life gives rise are as much tools as are windmills and spinning-wheels.

It follows that social and moral truths have no general validity, but are valid only for the society in which they arise. The nature of these truths will depend upon the nature of society, and the nature of society will depend upon the stage of technological development it has attained to.

Marx conceives this development in Hegelian terms, but substitutes the material world for the world spirit. In Hegel, the world spirit progressively reveals itself in dialectical stages through the conflict of ideas and dominant attitudes current at this or that stage of history. In Marx, the conflict is between classes. The dominating class constitutes the thesis, the dominated class the antithesis. Their conflict produces, not the victory of one or the other, but a new form of society which can be regarded as a synthesis of the two opposing classes. This new synthesis constitutes a new dominating class which produces its own antithesis in the class it dominates, and this leads to a fresh conflict and the evolution of another new form of society. This process will end when the class which embodies the interests of mankind in general and not of any section of it comes out on top: it will not constitute a new oppressing class, since there will be no one excluded from it to oppress, and the dialectical spiral will cease. This is the "dialectical" part of Marx's philosophy.

Marx was not a technical philosopher and the philosophy of dialectical materialism derives from scattered writings and from the writing of Friedrich Engels (1820-1895), who presented this philosophy in a more orderly way.

8

MARXISM IS a kind of inverted idealism. Hegelian idealism the right way up was a very powerful influence in England during the latter half of the nineteeth century, submerging for a time the empirical tradition native to this country. Thomas Hill Green (1836-1882) adopted Hegel's concept of the Absolute as the solution of the mind-matter problem. He rejected Kant's duality of appearance—the world as found in the mind—and reality—the world as it is in itself—in favour of a distinction between human and limited mind and absolute and unlimited mind, the former producing "appearance", the latter constituting "reality". Francis Herbert Bradley (1846-1924)—usually considered the major English philosopher of this period—was driven by an exceedingly acute critical faculty to a form of idealism close to Hegel's. In his chief work, *Appearance and Reality*, he demonstrates that all the general categories of thought involve irresolvable contradictions if they are assumed to be descriptions of reality. They must therefore belong to the plane of appearance, and reality must be an absolute transcending all categories of thought. Bernard Bosanquet (1848-1923) produced a philosophical system derived from Hegel, and the metaphysical system of John Ellis McTaggart (1866-1925), expounded in *The Nature of Existence*—one of the classics of reasoning in English—is idealist in character. The principal idealist in America during the period was Josiah Royce (1855-1916), who sought to prove idealism the only logically tenable philosophic position.

These names are only the greatest among an entire generation of philosophers for whom Hegelian idealism in one form or another all but constituted philosophy as such. It was a period in which two millennia of philosophical questioning seemed to have been crowned with an answer. Rationalism and empiricism had begotten Kant; Kant and his contemporary critics had begotten Hegel; and Hegel had begotten the truth. When the reaction to this arrived it arrived in a violent form— or rather, in two violent forms: two revolts against, not only idealism, but against philosophy as such, as it had been understood hitherto.

9

BEFORE EXAMINING the modern positivist and existentialist revolts against traditional philosophy, we must take a look at the reaction to idealism called "pragmatism", which appears, in retrospect, as a sort of preliminary to the full-scale twentieth century reaction. The term was introduced into philosophy by the American logician Charles Sanders Peirce (1839-1914) and later employed with a different meaning by William James (1842-1910) and John Dewey (1859-1952). Peirce employed it as the name of a logical maxim designed to determine the meaning of concepts. He said that if we could define all the experimental phenomena which would be implied by a concept, we would have obtained a complete definition of the concept. For a concept to have meaning it is necessary that experiments can be made which will define it. We can define "soft", for example, by describing the experiments which would establish that some thing is soft: that it is easily indented, and so on. The totality of these experiments would define the meaning of "soft". Peirce considered that this principle demonstrated the meaninglessness of many metaphysical concepts, but he considered it a means for establishing meaning and not for determining truth, and he repudiated the employment of the term pragmatism to denote a theory of truth. Peirce's definition of the term is now obsolete, and the sense given it by, above all, William James, is that currently accepted.

By pragmatism, James meant the theory that what is true is what is good from a human point of view, and the ordinary meaning of the word today is that a theory or doctrine must be judged according to the results that follow from it. "Pragmatic" has come to mean the opposite of "dogmatic": to judge a theory pragmatically means to judge it according to the results it produces. The common employment of the word is undoubtedly useful and, in this sense, a pragmatic approach to practical affairs has a lot to commend it, but it should be made clear that James and other American philosophical pragmatists of the nineteeth century meant something rather more than this: they meant that if a belief led to good results, then that belief should be considered true. James referred to "the truth's cash-value in experimental terms" and he undoubtedly meant by this that the consequences of believing a thing true were to determine the validity of the belief. It is obvious that this definition of truth, whatever arguments can be adduced in its favour, conflicts with what almost all other philosophers, and indeed most men of any kind, have considered the correct definition of truth, that is to say, correspondence with fact. This criticism led Dewey to abandon the position that pragmatism was a theory of truth and he maintained that one should substitute the term "warranted assertibility" for the word "truth", and pragmatism is, in any event, no longer a viable philosophical position.

The foregoing does not by any means exhaust either the ramifications of the school of pragmatism or the scope of the philosophy of James or Dewey, who are the most notable American philosophers. It might have seemed at one time that in this school a philosophical tradition native to America had arrived, but this was not the case. Despite the great abilities of the many philosophers native to or working in the United States, and especially those of James and Dewey, no specifically American mode of philosophy has yet emerged which can be compared with the Greek tradition from Thales to Epicurus, the German tradition from Leibniz to Nietzsche, the French tradition from Descartes to Sartre, or the English tradition from Bacon to Bertrand Russell—which is not to say that the groundwork for such a specifically American tradition may not even now be in the process of formation.

10

PHILOSOPHY IN the twentieth century exists largely in two compartments, which may be called "positivism" and "existentialism". But these terms are hardly more than convenient lables, useful as an aid to distinguishing the main tendencies, but not capable of being defined in a way which would include all philosophers loosely called positivists or existentialists. Neither are these terms opposites (as might perhaps be thought on the analogy of empiricist and rationalist). They are rather complementary to one another, in that they deal not with the same area of experience in different ways, but with different areas of experience. And both involve a breach with philosophy as previously understood.

The proposition which unites all philosophers who can be called positivist is that all genuine knowledge is based on sense experience, and that metaphysical speculation can produce no genuine knowledge and must be abandoned in favour of the methods of science. The Positive Philosophy of Auguste Comte (1798-1857) was the first elaborate presentation of this thesis, but its origins can be found in Hume and Bacon. Its revival in the present century is undoubtedly due to the advance of science. On one hand, academic philosophy had become sterile and unproductive, and the prevailing idealist orthodoxy seemed to bear little relation to reality; on the other, science was every year acquiring new real knowledge of the world and its workings, and by reason of this knowledge gaining greater and greater mastery over man's environment. In these circumstances, it was inevitable that younger philosophers should attempt to align the methods of philosophy with the methods of science, since these seemed self-evidently the true route to actual understanding. The outcome was not so much an increased emphasis upon the descriptive and analytical aspects of philosophy as the rejection of all philosophical activity which was not description or analysis. Three modern forms of positivism are important: logical atomism, logical positivism and linguistic analysis. Only a suggestion of their basic characteristics need be given here.

Logical atomism rests upon the new logic developed by Bertrand Russell and Alfred North Whitehead in *Principia Mathematica* of which a hint has been given in the section on logic in Part One. The aim is to show that logic, mathematics and language are structurally identical and that this structure corresponds with the structure of the world. By applying the principles of the new logic to linguistic statements, it is maintained, these statements can be rephrased in correct logical form, which is that of a simple subject-predicate sentence. This simple sentence is called an "atomic sentence", which means that it cannot be further broken down. For example, "Socrates is mortal" cannot be divided into any simpler sentences and is therefore an atomic sentence. But the sentence "All men are mortal" is capable of being rephrased as "Socrates is mortal", "Plato is mortal", "John is mortal", and so on until all individual men have been declared mortal. It is maintained that all sentences can be reduced to collections of atomic sentences which are identical in form with the axioms of logic and mathematics (which are themselves held to be identical). The result is a "theory of descriptions" through which, it is maintained, the structure of the real world can be described: it is composed, according to this theory, of an "atomic" fact (the subject) and a simple descriptive phrase (the predicate). This theory was stated in its most concise form by Ludwig Wittgenstein in his *Tractatus Logico-Philosophicus* (1922). Later, Wittgenstein repudiated this theory on the ground that although it appears to reject metaphysics it is itself metaphysical, inasmuch as it purports to provide facts about the real world on the basis of abstract logic.

It was for this reason, too, that the philosophers of the "Vienna Circle" who founded logical positivism also rejected logical atomism. Extremely dissatisfied with every philosophical position ever adopted, logical positivists maintained that the task of philosophy was not to produce propositions about the world but only to clarify the meaning of statements made by others. According to this outlook, there are three possible kinds of statement: logical (including mathematics), scientific (including statements of empirical observation) and nonsensical (including almost all philosophy hitherto). The object of classifying statements into one of these three kinds is to determine which discipline is appropriate for dealing with questions arising from it. Nonsensical propositions are held to be those which are not propositions of formal logic nor capable of being the subject of some scientific discipline: such propositions are not true or false, but literally without meaning, as a sentence of jibberish is without meaning. The criterion for distinguishing between a scientific proposition and a nonsensical one is called the principle of verifiability: a statement can be considered significant if one knows what observations would have to be made in order to verify or refute it; if no conceivable observation could either verify or refute a statement, it is without meaning. Thus the statement "All men have free will" is declared, not true or false, but meaningless, since no observation can be imagined which would verify or refute it.

Internal inconsistencies led to the decline of logical positivism, and contemporary positivism is represented by the school called linguistic analysis or ordinary language philosophy. In the view of ordinary language philosophers, it is still possible to make positive discoveries in philosophy, but not of the metaphysical kind. The philosopher's task is to understand the world through understanding the correct use of words. The analysis of language in terms of the use of words leads, it is claimed, to the correction of many misleading ideas. To understand how such words as "know", "believe", "promise" are actually used is to come nearer to a knowledge of the mind and of the nature of man. Philosophical perplexity is shown to arise in many cases not from any inherent difficulty in the subject-matter but in a subtle misuse of language, which suggests entities which have no real existence. For example, in his well-known book *The Concept of Mind*, Gilbert Ryle shows that many untenable ideas concerning the nature of the mind have arisen directly from the misunderstanding of how such words as "know, "believe" and "infer" are actually used.

The elevation of analysis of language to the position of being the chief concern of the philosopher has engendered, after passing through the stages of logical empiricism in the US and the school of linguistic analysis in Britain, the distinct discipline of semantics (i.e. the study of the relationship between words and that to which they refer). Semantics is now in process of following modern logic in hiving off from philosophy: in which process philosophy is again discharging its traditional function of being midwife to the other sciences.

Two distinguishing characteristics can be discerned in all these forms of positivism. Firstly, the big questions which are the subject of traditional philosophy are seemingly neglected in favour of smaller, particular problems; at the same time the big questions are declared to be meaningless. Secondly, positivism claims to make definite discoveries about the world which cannot be refuted in the way in which previous philosophical theories have been refutable. It is maintained, for instance, that the discovery that mistakes concerning the nature of mind arise from misunderstanding of the way in which such words as "know" and infer" are used in ordinary speech is a piece of knowledge quite different from a philosophical theory of the old sort. In both these respects positivism seeks to supplement science and, so to speak, justify the existence of philosophy as a practical activity.

This last consideration seems, indeed, to have been decisive for the whole development: one had to make of philosophy a discipline which could stand up for itself in the modern world, something firm and precise, something that could be undertaken, "done", as one "does" chemistry. The imposition of severe limitations is the first and most striking characteristic: limitation of subject matter, of breadth of reference, of interest, and of imagination—not because one does not wish to reflect on everything in life, but because everything in life is no longer potential subject matter for philosophy. Philosophy is analysis, description, a kind of science: it is not synthesis, invention, a kind of art. "A philosopher" is not a peculiar species of man, he is someone who does philosophy, as a chemist is someone who does chemistry. Above all, he is not a "lawgiver", he makes no claim to direction of the world—the pathos of the "great philosopher" such as adheres to Plato, Hegel, Marx, is repudiated. A philosopher is the practitioner of a certain discipline: that and no more.

II

IT WILL thus be seen that the other main philosophical movement of the present century, existentialism, is not an alternative to positivism but rather its complement. Existentialism deals with those areas of experience which are not only outside the province of traditional philosophy, but are also very evidently ignored by the positivist movement. Existentialism is not so much a single philosophical movement as a series of more or less violent expressions of dissatisfaction with traditional philosophy and with all other form of contemporary thought. Of the philosophers who have been called existentialist, only J.-P. Sartre accepts the label—but this is at least in part a consequence of the French penchant for banners and slogans.

The kind of breakaway from the philosophical tradition which can be labelled existentialist originates with Søren Kierkegaard (1813-1855) and Friedrich Nietzsche (1844-1900). Kierkegaard, who was a theologian rather than a philosopher, reacted violently against what he took to be the Hegelianism of mid-nineteenth century philosophy because it seemed to him to offer no guide to practical living. Whether Hegel was right or wrong seemed to him to be irrelevant to the questions with which men were actually concerned in their lives. The central question was about the meaning of existence and this question was prompted by the fact that, to the unaided reason, existence appeared to be without meaning. Problems of the nature of humanity, of life and of the world affected everyone, yet traditional philosophy provided no answer to them. Kierkegaard's answer was that to be human was to be placed in a frightening and anguishing predicament: that mankind was partly animal and partly a rational being was an irresolvable

K

paradox, and much of Kierkegaard's writing is concerned with elaborating the paradoxial nature of man. Because traditional philosophy was irrelevant to the immediate problems and interests of men, he proposed abandoning it, and with it all attempt to understand by reason. Instead he proposed a "leap" into belief in the irrational doctrines of Christianity, and his undertaking then was not to answer the question "Is Christianity true?" but the question "How can one live as a Christian?"

Most succeeding existentialists have not been Christians. What they have taken from Kierkegaard is his claim that to be a man is to be faced with an inexplicable universe in which the world around one, one's own nature, and the nature of being itself are such as to inspire anxiety.

Nietzsche, who knew nothing of Kierkegaard, faced nonetheless the same problem as he. To Nietzsche, all truth except scientific truth had been "unmasked" as error: a metaphysical, religious, moral or rational "truth" was true only from a certain perspective—considered absolutely it was false. Scientific truths, however, were, or purported to be, purely factual, and could give no information as to the *meaning* of the world: science answered the question "why?" only in the sense of "from what cause?" and never in the sense of "to what end?" The latter question no longer received any reply.

Unlike Kierkegaard, Nietzsche dealt with this situation, not by an effort of faith, but by pushing forward along the path of destruction until he had produced an anticipatory account of what he took to be the immediately impending condition of Western man, which he termed "nihilism". Nihilism, in Nietzsche's usage, means the belief that nothing is true or possesses value, and that the world and mankind are senseles: mankind, Nietzsche thought, was already on the road to that state of mind, and would have to attain it before sufficient strength could be engendered to overcome it—only a total and real scepticism could produce the forms of its own transcendence. The form of transcendence he himself produced, of which the "superman" is the embodiment and "will to power" the motive force, are not relevant to his role as a forerunner of existentialism: what is vital here is his "nihilistic" attack on all existing "truths".

Kierkegaard and Nietzsche were both great stylists in their respective languages, though their styles are very different from one another. Kierkegaard can be extremely prolix and the quality of his writing varies greatly from book to book and within the same book: he needs to be read in selections. Nietzsche, on the other hand, is always concise, and his standard is consistently high: he should be read in quantity if the sense of what he is saying is to become apparent—selective reading will distort it.

Historically speaking, Nietzsche's forecast of a nihilistic collapse in Europe seems to have been correct. It is scarcely possible in the world of today to believe that traditional philosophy has proved capable of affecting the actions of men in any but a superficial way. And with the decline in religious belief the absence of a living philosophical tradition leaves a vacuum corresponding to the nihilism Nietzsche predicted for the twentieth century. Existentialism is the response of philosophy to its own breakdown. The all-embracing system exemplified by Hegel's seems to be not so much out of date as irrelevant to the ends philosophy ought to serve. One of these ends is the assistance of science and the promotion of the greatest possible clarity in thinking, and this end is served by the various positivist schools. But philosophy has always had the task, not only of examining modes of thought and sources of knowledge, but also of examining what can vaguely be called "the human condition". This side of philosophy, represented in the past by metaphysical and ethical systems, is represented in the present by existentialism.

What is existentialism? J.-P. Sartre defined it—and this is indeed the definition of the *word*—as the doctrine that in the case of man existence precedes essence. The essence of a thing, the reader may or may not recall from our brief discussion of Aquinas, is its essential nature, that which it essentially is; its existence is the actualisation of this essence. The existence of a hammer, for example, is, together with its form and size, dependent on the idea of it in the mind of its maker: the idea of it, which is its essence, precedes its existence. But man, it is maintained, exists without the idea of "man" having preceded him: man is here, in the world, but his "essence" is nowhere. What follows? That he himself *makes* his essence in the course of his existence—as Nietzsche puts it, "man is the animal *whose nature has not been fixed*" and who is thus not merely free to create his own nature but actually compelled to do so every time he acts. Compulsion to be free is the source of the anxiety which is Kierkegaard's constant theme.

There is clearly some connection between this definition and that of Karl Jaspers, who said that existentialism is "a philosophy which does not cognize objects" but "elucidates and makes actual the being of the thinker"—a philosophy that is not a science but rather a mode of self-evolution. Jaspers is in general concerned to stress the unscientific character of philosophy as he understands it, thus setting his brand in diametrical opposition to the positivist schools. It was Jaspers, too, who wrote that the contemporary philosophical situation "is determined by the fact that two philosophers, Kierkegaard and Nietzsche, who did not count in their times . . . have continually grown in significance"—which is, of course, the contemporary philosophical situation seen from a completely different angle from that from which it is seen by the followers of Russell and Moore.

Martin Heidegger, the third of the most famous "existentialists", objected to that term to characterise his own philosophy on the ground that, while Sartre's definition was certainly correct, to say that "existence precedes essence" is still to speak the language of metaphysics, and he, Heidegger, believed metaphysics to be impossible. To Heidegger, Nietzsche was the "last metaphysician of the West" who had demonstrated the impossibility of metaphysics: Heidegger's study is ontology—the nature of being—and human existence he regards as a "window" through which being can be observed.

Much of what existentialist philosophers reflect on is also

within the province of poetry, drama and the novel, namely human emotions, fears, anxieties and passions, and some of the notorious difficulty of their writings originates in the effort to discuss such things in the language of philosophy.

To make clear what is implied, let us take the following problem. A child runs into the road and is knocked down and killed by a car. What sense is there in this event? If the nature of human life is such that its existence can be negated by a seemingly senseless occurrence, what conclusions can one draw about it? To this question traditional philosophy supplies no answer. Indeed, it seems that the whole incident lies outside the world in which traditional philosophy exists. To the modern positivist, the question will be without significance. It is of a kind which, from the positivist point of view, cannot be raised, whether because its answer would be beyond the competence of philosophy, or because the question is literally meaningless. Now, it is with the problems posed by precisely the kind of event represented by a child's being knocked down and killed by a car that existentialism is concerned.

The relevance of positivism to ordinary behaviour and to the manifold problems of day-to-day existence is problematical. But then positivism does not pretend to be concerned with such problems: the positivist aim is to make limited but precise discoveries in the realms of language, thought and science. One does not criticise a dentist because he cannot cure cancer, and we should not criticise a positivist because he cannot explain the meaning of life. From the other point of view, the relevance of existentialism to the problems of everyday life is supreme and obvious. But this relevance is maintained at some cost, principally the relinquishment of the very important project undertaken by positivist thinkers to produce definite results, actual discoveries and irreversible advances in philosophical thinking. Again, it may be said that one should not criticise a philosopher for failing to do what he does not set out to do. The problems which are the subject-matter of existentialism are probably incapable of precise formulation, let alone precise solution.

As one might expect, then, both movements have their advantages and achievements, both their disadvantages and failures. Neither corresponds to what has up to the present century been considered philosophy, but each corresponds to an aspect of it. We have already seen that the "reasoning" part of philosophy—that concerned with logic and knowledge—does not unite very comfortably with the "behaviour" part—that concerned with ethics and morals. The present division between positivism and existentialism represents in some measure a division between these two parts of philosophy. Only rarely in the past have they been fused into a satisfying and comprehensive whole, and it is not easy to see how the thing is to be done again, or whether there is in reality any firm ground between the positivist and existentialist camps. Yet it is only from a union of rigorous thinking with a concern for the questions which perplex and sometimes terrify men in their ordinary lives that philosophy in the comprehensive sense can be reborn.

BIBLIOGRAPHY

H. P. Rickman: *Preface to Philosophy* (Routledge and Kegan Paul). An undogmatic introduction to the subject-matter of philosophy.

Karl Jaspers: *Philosophy is for Everyman* (Hutchinson). Described by its subtitle as "a short course in philosophical thinking": its value lies in the impression it conveys that philosophy is worth doing.

John Passmore: *A Hundred Years of Philosophy* (Duckworth, Penguin). "A masterpiece of digestion and exposition" the TLS said, and so it is. Not particularly easy, but make your way carefully and if you are not gripped by it then philosophy is probably not for you.

A. J. Ayer: *The Central Questions of Philosophy* (Weidenfeld & Nicolson, Penguin). Lectures on the subjects which chiefly concern British and American philosophers.

A. A. Luce: *Logic* (Teach Yourself Books, English UP). A good introduction to formal logic.

G. E. Moore: *Ethics* (OUP). A classic exposition of the problems of ethics.

The Cosmological Arguments, ed. Donald R. Burrill (Anchor Books). "Is there rational evidence for the existence of God?"—an excellent anthology of discussions of this question from Plato onwards.

Bryan Magee: *Modern British Philosophy* (Paladin). Edited transcripts of radio conversations between Magee and 13 British philosophers: good and interesting talk, out of which emerges a clear impression of the current state of British philosophy.

Existentialism from Dostoevsky to Sartre, ed. Walter Kaufmann (Meridian Books). Well chosen anthology of existentialist and allied writers, with commentary.

Plato: *The Last Days of Socrates*, trs. Hugh Tredennick; *The Symposium*, trs. Walter Hamilton; *Gogias*, trs. Walter Hamilton; *Protagoras* and *Meno*, trs. W. K. C. Guthrie; *The Republic*, trs. H. D. P. Lee; *Timaeus* and *Critias*, trs. H. D. P. Lee; *The Laws*, trs. Trevor J. Saunders (Penguin). All are furnished with introductions and notes. Read them as you would any other books; don't anticipate difficulties.

Descartes: *Discourse on Method* and the *Meditations*, trs. F. E. Sutcliffe (Penguin). The same remarks apply. The point is to read a few *philosophical texts* and discover what your reaction is, how much you understand and fail to understand, etc.

David Hume: *A Treatise of Human Nature*, ed. Ernest C. Mossner (Penguin). Harder going, but the style is superb: philosophy written in ordinary (18th century) English.

Bertrand Russell: *An Inquiry into Meaning and Truth* (Penguin). Harder than Hume, but attempt it; don't anticipate difficulties you may not find.

The Concise Encyclopaedia of Western Philosophy, ed. J. O. Urmson (Hutchinson). A highly readable reference book.

INDEX